Coordinating Special Educational Needs

Coordinating Special Educational Needs

A Guide for the Early Years

Damien Fitzgerald

continuum

KH

Continuum International Publishing Group

The Tower Building
11 York Road
SE1 7NX

80 Maiden Lane, Suite 704
New York, NY 10038

www.continuumbooks.com

British Library Cataloguing-in-Publication Data
A catalogue record for this book is available from the British Library.

ISBN: 082648476X (paperback)

Library of Congress Cataloging-in-Publication Data
A catalog record for this book is available from the Library of Congress.

Typeset by Fakenham Photosetting Ltd
Printed and bound in Great Britain by Ashford Colour Press, Gosport, Hampshire

7/29/08

Contents

Contents

Contents

Introduction

There have been increasing levels of recognition and support for children with special educational needs (SEN) in recent years. A range of legislation and the introduction of the Special Educational Needs Code of Practice (SENCOP) (DfES 1994, 2001a) have underpinned the development of support for children with learning difficulties across the range of educational provision. This development has been based on a set of principles that emphasize partnership with parents and children, and between early years settings, schools, the local authority (LA) and other agencies, as key factors in supporting effective service delivery to children with SEN and their families.

Within the code of practice different areas of learning difficulties have been identified. These areas are, however, interlinked and it is acknowledged that there is 'a wide spectrum of special educational needs that are frequently interrelated' (DfES 2001a: 7:52). The four areas of SEN and requirements are identified as:

♦ Communication and interaction

♦ Cognition and learning

♦ Behaviour, emotional and social development

♦ Sensory and/or physical needs

Introduction

Medical conditions are also included, although it is made clear that a medical condition does not in itself mean that a child has SEN. Instead, it is the impact of the condition (either directly because of the condition or indirectly because of the psychological impact of illness, treatment or other aspects of the condition) on the child's learning ability, social and behavioural development that may lead to the SEN.

This book is mainly concerned with the coordination of special educational needs and how this can be approached within early years settings. As such, discussion within this book may stray outside these settings to reflect the complex and interrelated nature of SEN and how they involve work with children, families and practitioners within a setting, and with other multi-professional teams. The role of the Special Educational Needs Coordinator (SENCO) will be explored. There is also an overview of the legislation that relates to SEN; voluntary, independent, private and state settings are all increasingly being expected to show how they take due account of relevant legislation, policy and codes of practice. The impact of intervention on the child and family will be explored and strategies to ensure that the views of children and families are taken account of in decision-making processes will also be discussed.

Within the key themes – the role of the SENCO, working with others, and supporting the child and family – there will be discussion of how the management and coordination of special needs is best undertaken to assist readers with identifying areas for potential development. The book also includes discussion of the changing expectations of Special Educational Needs Coordinators (SENCOs), and aims to identify potential future challenges and how these could contribute to more positive outcomes for children and families, and enhance the role and status of practitioners. The book is organized in two parts. The first, Chapters 1–4, provides background information on how the role has developed, legislative implications and discussion of working with children and parents. The second, Chapters 5–8, provides practical guidance on different parts of the SENCO role with the aim of supporting practitioners who are considering taking on this role or those who are currently in the position and are looking to develop their working practices further.

This book is aimed at SENCOs, early years practitioners, their managers and tutors on early years courses. The book will also be of interest to students who work with children and those hoping to move into a SENCO role in the future. In the context of this book, 'early years' will refer to children aged 0–8 years old in children's centres, nurseries, pre-schools, school, in a home-based setting and in any other setting where children spend time. 'Early years practitioner' refers to anyone working in these types of settings in any capacity, and could include teachers, teaching assistants, nursery nurses, playworkers, pre-school workers and volunteers. In this book you will find case studies to illustrate some of the issues raised; points for reflection or discussion; self-assessment exercises; and action points to encourage you to gather information or resources to help you develop your skills in supporting children with SEN. These aspects of the book are intended to help you extend your understanding and to reflect on your own stage of development in this area. There is also a list of references and further reading at the end of the book for those who wish to extend their knowledge and understanding of children with SEN. Throughout the book the terms 'she' and 'he' are used randomly to avoid the more clumsy s/he and him/her.

Part 1
Setting the Context

1

The Role of the SENCO

Introduction

The role of the SENCO can be difficult to understand, partly because it can vary significantly between settings. This chapter outlines how the role developed in relation to the Special Education Need Codes of Practice (1994 and 2001) and discusses key aspects of the role. The aim of the chapter is to assist SENCOs, or those interested in becoming a SENCO, in thinking reflectively about the role and identifying some areas where changes in working practices or procedures could lead to more effective outcomes for practitioners and children. To assist with this, the final activity of the chapter uses an action-planning approach that you will find useful. Action planning should not be seen as a one-off activity but something that you reflect on and amend as necessary (Schon 1983). Chapters 5–8 of the book will also be useful in supporting this process by suggesting approaches to practice that can be incorporated as part of your action plan.

How the SENCO role developed and what it involves

All private, voluntary and state providers of early education who receive government funding are required to have a designated person who is responsible for coordinating the setting's activities around special educational needs. The idea of having a 'specialist' taking responsibility for coordinating provision for children with special educational needs came about for schools with the introduction of the 1994 Code of Practice (DFE 1994) and from this the role of SENCO emerged. This was extended to non-school based settings providing full day care in 2001 (OfSTED 2001). For example, the day-care standards set out expectations that at least one member of staff:

◆ Has knowledge of the Special Educational Needs Code of Practice (SENCOP)

◆ Keeps relevant records to support the ongoing development of children with a SEN

◆ Produces a policy on how the setting provides for children with a SEN.

The expectations of early years settings were further emphasized with the publication in 2004 of *Removing Barriers to Achievement*, which highlighted the need for early intervention to improve the provision and management of SEN (DfES 2004a).

Activity

In addition to the way each person organizes their role it is important to consider the skills that a person needs to be an effective SENCO. Think about your role as SENCO (or someone who you know who is a SENCO) and make a list of the skills that you think they need to carry out the role.

Although the SENCOP provides guidance, this does not necessarily make it clear what the role of a SENCO involves. If you were to gather a group of SENCOs together and ask them to describe their role there would be many variations. Some of this variation can be explained by the type and size of the setting. These differences are just one of the factors that can seem to make the role seem difficult as there is no one approach or way of doing things that can be given to a new SENCO as 'the best' way of doing the job. In some settings the SENCO will be a member of the management team and the role may be one of many management responsibilities. In others the role may be allocated and might shift between people who show a particular interest in the subject. Some SENCOs will spend a significant amount of time working directly with children with SEN, either one-to-one, in small group situations or as part of the group or class. In contrast, some SENCOs, particularly in larger settings, may not work directly with children themselves but instead take a coordinating role in planning, organizing and supporting members of the team who do work with those children with specific needs. For SENCOs, particularly if new to the role, this can seem daunting but it can also mean that there is scope for each SENCO to develop their role in a way that best suits the setting and fully utilizes the range of skills and abilities of practitioners in the setting.

It is likely that your list for the previous activity will have included a wide variety of skills such as the ability to:

◆ Work well with practitioners from multiple agencies

Coordinating SEN

- Establish good relationships with children, parents and colleagues
- Devise and manage systems to implement and track the progress of educational plans for a number of children
- Respond to requests for verbal and written information in a timely way
- Write reports and letters for a variety of audiences
- Track how resources are used and prepare requests for additional resources from money that is part of the setting budget and from outside agencies
- Organize and coordinate meetings, including the distribution of relevant information and documents prior to and after the meeting
- Able to prioritize and organize available resources in a way that best provides for the interests of all children
- Provide advice and support for colleagues to develop their knowledge of SEN and enable them to meet the needs of each child
- Attend meetings and committees to represent children, families and the setting in a variety of forums
- Participate in ongoing professional development to remain aware of current practices, new developments and ensure that new requirements and approaches are implemented efficiently and effectively.

As stated earlier, this can seem daunting but it is important to remember that providing for children with SENs is the responsibility of each practitioner, a point clearly made in the code of practice (DfES 2001a). The SENCO does have a role in coordinating these activities but should not be expected to take full responsibility for every child with special needs. The challenge for each SENCO is to find ways of managing the role rather than the role managing you.

Whether you have been a SENCO for some time, are new to the role or interested in understanding more about it, there are a number of things that you can do (or reflect on) to ensure that you feel and are seen by your colleagues as being effective in your role. There is always a tendency with a busy role to think that time spent reviewing what you do and the systems in place is wasted time as you are not actually producing something. But this is not the case. It is generally well understood, whether related to your personal life, career, educational goals or a specific issue, that time reflecting is time well spent (Atkins and Murphy 1994). To assist with this process it can be helpful to divide the role of the SENCO into six broad areas:

♦ Administration systems

♦ Tracking and monitoring systems

♦ Liaising with multi-agency professionals

♦ Continuing professional development for practitioners

♦ Professional development for SENCOs (self)

♦ Working with parents.

This list is not intended to cover all aspects of the role but it does offer a starting point for thinking about how you manage what are likely to be significant components of each area. Working with parents is a particularly important part of the SENCO role and is covered in Chapter 3. The following sections provide a brief overview of some key issues for each area, followed by reflection points to help you think about the way these are managed in your own setting.

Administration systems

All SENCOs will find themselves on the receiving end of a large volume of letters, reports, requests for meetings and general enquiries. To manage this efficiently it is important to have systems in place. Much of the communication may actually be requests that can be dealt with quickly by other people in the setting who have the information to hand, particularly in larger systems. In this way the volume of paperwork passed on to SENCOs will be reduced, requests will be answered quickly and the time you have available for the role can be utilized effectively.

Reflection

♦ Does the amount of time you spend dealing with administration reduce the amount of time you feel you should spend on other aspects of your role?

♦ Do you have a system in place for recording

correspondence, requests for meetings and messages that are taken on your behalf or initially seen by others (this could be as simple as a box file in an office where requests are dated and stored)?

♦ Are there requests for information that can be dealt with by colleagues and do you have a system in place for communicating when the information is required by and ensuring it is completed?

♦ Do you have a specific allocation of time that you keep free each week to deal with administration tasks?

♦ Is necessary information clearly communicated to relevant colleagues?

♦ Is there a confidential central filing system where relevant records for each child with special needs are stored so that information can be accessed efficiently and is kept up to date?

♦ Are colleagues aware of what records are kept centrally so that they know what information to pass on to ensure the record is complete and kept up to date?

♦ If maintaining these records and filing the information is time-consuming are you able to access support from colleagues to assist with this task?

Tracking and monitoring systems

An important but often time-consuming and difficult task for SENCOs is keeping track of each child with special educational needs so that they can get the best support possible. This will involve monitoring individual educational plans, evaluating actions to plan for the next stage, organizing review meetings, following up on agreed actions and ensuring that the child, parents and other professionals are consulted and informed of any decisions (Cole 2005). For children who are supported by external agencies, this may also include completing reports required as part of the special needs process (e.g. for decisions about moving between stages of the special needs code or in decisions linked to issuing a statement of special educational needs). Another reason why it is important to have efficient systems in place for tracking past stages and decisions is that requests for information linked to statutory processes will have set time limits by which a response is expected.

Reflection

♦ Is there a clear record in place that details the name of each child with special educational needs, their stage in the code of practice, their next review data and comments about required actions?

♦ Are you making the best use of ICT systems to assist with tracking (e.g. spreadsheet) and producing required documentation such as Individual Educational Plans (IEPs), standard letters and reports?

♦ Are there opportunities for parents to meet with practitioners to discuss issues that may arise between reviews and to respond to questions at an early stage, thus preventing issues escalating?

♦ Is the best use made of resources and outside professionals to support each child and ensure that decisions are made quickly and appropriate evaluation carried out to promote ongoing progress?

Professional development for practitioners

An ongoing challenge for all practitioners is to keep up to date with the breadth of physical, emotional, social and psychological conditions that can impact on development. For teachers, this expectation is set out in the revised draft standards, which teachers will be expected to attain to gain qualified status (Teacher Development Agency 2006). For voluntary, independent and private settings the full day-care national standards state that practitioners need to, 'have a secure knowledge and understanding of the individual needs of every child in their care' (OfSTED 2001: 43). It is not reasonable to expect every practitioner to have detailed knowledge of every condition that children may come to a setting with or develop while they are there. It is important though that practitioners, with support from the setting SENCO, are able to get access to information and support they need to ensure that each child can receive appropriate education and care, and to ensure they make ongoing progress and reach their potential.

In some settings the SENCO will take a key role in supporting the ongoing professional development of practitioners in relation to understanding special needs and disability issues. This could be in the form of taking responsibility for designing and delivering programmes of training, taking line management responsibility for a team of practitioners, allocating practitioners to work with individual or groups of children, or overseeing the allocation and coordination of professional development courses delivered by external agencies. This is more likely to form part of a SENCO's role in a large setting, such as a children's centre with varied early years provision, or a school. In other settings the SENCO may not have any direct responsibility for ongoing professional development of practitioners, or line management responsibilities. This latter approach can be problematic, even in smaller settings and is not in line with guidance contained in the Code of Practice (DfES 2001a), which states that SENCOs should be part of the management team.

If, as SENCO, you have responsibility for the line management and support of other practitioners it is important to take a systematic and organized approach to this aspect of the role. To be effective Gerschel (2005) summarizes a number of strategies that lead to the effective management of practitioners who support children with SEN:

♦ A clear organizational strategy within the setting, with clearly defined roles for practitioners and the SENCO

♦ Active support, training and direction from relevant bodies (such as the Local Authority, Childcare Coordinator, Children's Trust or local Sure Start schemes)

♦ The SENCO takes responsibility for day-to-day organization of SEN resources. Depending on the setting, this could include deployment of practitioners and allocation of roles

♦ A system for supporting and advising all practitioners within the setting to support each child effectively

♦ The SENCO takes responsibility for induction and training.

Over recent years there has been a significant expansion in the range and level of qualifications to support early years practitioners' professional development. These could be in the form of:

♦ Certificated training from local authorities, Children's Trusts or other providers

♦ National Vocational Qualifications (NVQs)

♦ Foundation Degrees (practice focused)

♦ Honours degrees, which often include an element of practice based training.

Research highlights the significant benefits to practitioners who enhance their level of qualification as the higher the qualification level, the better the outcomes for children (Sylva *et al.* 2004). A ten-year strategy from the government supports this by stating the intention to enhance the qualification base of staff and ensure that each setting contains at least one graduate (HM Treasury *et al.* 2004). There is likely to be greater emphasis on this now as there is a clear commitment through the Children's Workforce Network, coordinated by The Children's Workforce Development Council (CWDC), to improve the training and qualifications base for practitioners who work with children (CWDC 2006a, DfES 2006).

Reflection

♦ Do you have access to a designated special needs budget to support the professional development of practitioners in your setting?

♦ If practitioners want to gain a qualification to enhance their knowledge and skills are you able to support them to find relevant training?

♦ Are there opportunities for practitioners to attend in-service development events to increase their knowledge and understanding of special needs?

♦ Are you aware of national and local funding opportunities that practitioners from your setting may be able to access to support their continuing professional development?

Professional development for SENCOs (or self)

For SENCOs to carry out their role effectively, work openly with parents and be able to offer support to colleagues, it is vital that they have a good level of knowledge and skills (Gerschel 2005). This knowledge is likely to be gained over a period of time so careful thought needs to be given to when you agree to take on the role of SENCO (if this is relevant to you). This will vary from person to person and you should take account of how much previous experience and training you have in relation to special needs. Another important factor to consider is the experience you have gained that will enable you to manage complex administration systems, liaise with multi-disciplinary professionals and communicate in writing and verbally. To be effective you do not need to know about every special need but it is important to have a broad knowledge of the range of special needs children are likely to have in your setting.

In addition to gaining practical experience, many of the tasks connected with the SENCO role reflect the expectations set out in the standards for achieving Early Years Professional (EYP) status. The standards for achieving the status have been developed by the Children's Workforce Development Council (CWDC) and there is an expectation that all full and sessional day-care settings will have practitioners with EYP status in place over the coming years. The aim of the status is to develop a workforce, as set out in *Every Child Matters*, that holds relevant experience, skills and knowledge of relevant theory to inform their practice (CWDC 2006b), to ensure that each child is supported effectively and to meet the Children Act (2004). To achieve the status practitioners may need additional training (this will vary according to past training and experience) and will have to go through a validation process with a training provider, which will include reflecting on your practice and showing how you have implemented change (CWDC 2006c). As part of this, practitioners will have to reflect on their practice and make links with theory and policy to show how they meet the standards.

Many of the tasks associated with the role of SENCO link with the standards, which provide a sound basis for supporting ongoing professional development. For example, a SENCO is likely to be able to demonstrate evidence of how their practice meets many of the expectations necessary to gain EYP status, as shown by the exemplar extracts from the standards below:

♦ Awareness of policies for safeguarding and promoting the well-being of children

♦ Awareness of contributions that others can make to the physical and emotional well-being of children [i.e. as SENCO offering support and guidance to other practitioners]

♦ High expectations of all children and a commitment to ensuring they can achieve their full potential

♦ Promote inclusion and anti-discriminatory practice

♦ Listen to children, pay attention to what they say and value and respect their views

♦ Work in partnership with families and develop constructive relationships

♦ Establish a system and culture of collaboration and cooperative working among colleagues

♦ Contribute to the work of multi-professional teams and coordinate and implement agreed programmes of intervention.

It is also important that practitioners remain aware of new and ongoing developments in the special needs process so that systems take account of statutory and local expectations to meet the needs of children with SEN. Layton (2005) emphasizes the importance of SENCOs having an ongoing commitment to continuing professional development and this should include taking some responsibility for leadership of special needs within the setting. Part of this responsibility should include contributing to the support of colleagues in their development. To enable this to happen it is important that when discussing professional development (i.e. with an appraiser, mentor or line manager), this should include attention to the development of management and leadership skills for SENCOs to carry out these functions in a way that is appropriate to each individual setting.

This variety in the SENCO role makes it both interesting and challenging; although, as the range of tasks is broad this can often make the role overly demanding. If you want to develop processes, procedures and practices to provide effective support for all children with SEN the devising of an action plan can be useful.

Activity

At this point it would be useful to spend some time completing the action plan. This activity will be useful in providing a starting point for reviewing four of the key areas in the context of your own development and setting, if that is relevant to you. The following template does not cover action and plans related to *working with parents* or *liaising with multi-agency professionals* as these are covered in Chapters 3 and 8 respectively. The following points will help you to reflect on each of the areas:

♦ Think about the four areas discussed in this chapter and make some brief notes about what you see as the strengths and areas for development in your setting. As part of this process talk to colleagues, external specialists and parents as they will be able to offer different perspectives.

♦ Make some notes on the actions that would be necessary to develop each area.

♦ If there are a number of areas for development (which there may well be) think about which of the actions are a priority. When deciding what actions to prioritize it is useful to think about the actions that are most likely to bring about the most significant improvements relatively quickly.

♦ Discuss the identified priorities with the management team to gain their support and to ensure that any necessary resources are available to enable the changes to be made.

♦ Communicate the changes to colleagues to ensure they are informed and able to offer feedback, and to gain their support with implementing the identified actions.

♦ Set a clear timetable for implementing the changes that takes account of other demands that are taking place within your setting.

- ◆ Think about how the changes can be evaluated. Try to keep this simple and ensure that adequate time has been given to implement the changes before starting the evaluation.
- ◆ If there are other changes that need to be implemented this process can be repeated.

Administration Systems		
Strengths	Areas for development	Actions for development

Tracking and Monitoring Systems		
Strengths	Areas for development	Actions for development

Professional Development for Practitioners		
Strengths	Areas for development	Actions for development

Professional Development for SENCO (or self)		
Strengths	Areas for development	Actions for development

Conclusion

This chapter, in discussing the broad aspects of the role of the SENCO, has also highlighted the differences that may occur between different settings. In some settings the SENCO may work with children in much the same way as other practitioners, and in others their sole role may be taken up with supporting other practitioners, managing resources and maintaining effective communication systems to ensure that the requirements of the SEN Code of Practice are met. This is what makes the role of the SENCO both challenging and interesting. It is possible to think how the role can be developed within your setting or how you would approach it if you are not currently a SENCO. The activities in this chapter are intended as a starting point to assist with this process. The subsequent chapters will provide information and explore more strategies for ensuring that the role of the SENCO is manageable, effective and organized in a way that best supports other practitioners and meets the needs of each child with an SEN and their families.

2

Legislation and Guidance: What SENCOs need to know

There is a range of legislation and guidance documents that set out expectations in relation to the provision of services for children with special needs. Some of the legislation and guidance has a direct impact on special needs processes and practice. Other legislation, although not directly focused on special needs, may impact on practice and it will be useful to be familiar with the key elements of this. This chapter will provide an overview of the range of legislation that SENCOs and practitioners need to be aware of or may hear about in their day-to-day work. Often, when discussing legislation, SENCOs and other practitioners become concerned that they do not understand every element of the guidance, but this is not necessary. If a detailed understanding of how a piece of legislation or guidance impacts on a specific issue is needed then advice will be available from others, such as Local Authority officers, Policy officers or Special Needs Advisors (the title of these will vary in different areas). If required, there should also be access to advice from legal practitioners, although this is not likely to be required on a regular basis. The overall aim of this chapter is to give an overview of some relevant legislation and guidance so that practitioners feel more familiar with how this feeds into practice and procedure and aims to ensure equitable access for all children and families.

Special Educational Needs Code of Practice (SENCOP)

The main document that SENCOs are likely to refer to for guidance on procedures and practice is the SENCOP (DfES 2001a). The SENCOP is what it says – a *code* of practice. So in a literal sense the code is not a statutory document. The Act, which is formed when a Bill receives Royal Assent following its passage through Parliament is, in contrast, a statutory requirement that sets out the legal expectations of relevant settings. The language that Acts are written in is usually complex and contains many legal terms that would be difficult for non-legal professionals to follow. So, to assist early years settings (and other educational establishments) and practitioners, a code of practice is produced. This sets out, in clear language, what the legal requirements are for early years settings, which when followed, will mean that they are acting in accordance with the legal expectations of the relevant Act(s).

The 2001 SENCOP signalled a move away from the often cumbersome and bureaucratic statementing process (Farrell 2001). It suggested a graduated approach to supporting children with a special need to achieve greater inclusion for children and, as far as possible, ensure that they are educated alongside their peers. The SENCOP also signalled an expectation that more funding for special needs should be delegated to individual settings and this expectation was further reinforced by the DfES, alongside the need for health and social care services to work effectively with education providers to ensure early intervention and support (DfES 2004a). In response to this there has been a significant reduction in the number of statutory assessments in some authorities and children are now supported in other ways. For example, in some authorities a delegated audit system has been implemented in maintained nursery and primary schools. This allocates additional funding to children with a wide range of identified special needs without having to go through the full statutory assessment process, which is costly, can be demoralizing to parents and often results in relatively low levels of additional support being provided. For a child to be eligible for additional funding, settings have to ensure that they have followed the graduated approach and taken advice from external specialists and acted on it. As well as using resources more efficiently, this approach aims to increase the amount of time external specialists spend supporting rather than assessing children.

All providers that receive an element of government funding must take account of the SENCOP, which details expectations for children with SENs. A child is defined as having a SEN if they have a learning difficulty that is significantly greater than that of most children and requires special support. The Code sets out expectations to ensure that children with a SEN are not disadvantaged in terms of admission to a setting and that there is adequate provision and support for their need. There is also an expectation that the rights of children are a central part of decision-making and this is discussed in more depth in Chapter 4. Overall, the Code was informed by the following general principles:

♦ A child with special needs should have his needs met

♦ The special needs of children will normally be met in mainstream schools

♦ The views of children should be sought and taken into account

♦ Parents have a vital role to play in supporting their child's education

♦ Children with SEN should be offered full access to a broad, balanced and relevant education, including an appropriate curriculum for the foundation stage and the National Curriculum (Teachernet 2006).

A significant addition to the 2001 Code was specific reference to children in the early years. There are now two main stages that early years settings or schools work within. If concern still remains after this, a decision may be made to move to a statutory assessment. An overview of this process is provided in Figure 2.1. When decisions are being made about the stage a child is at and the next actions to take, one should always consider whether a child is able to move back a stage as well as forward. In some cases a child may enter an early years setting with a statement. This is only likely to apply to a relatively small number of children who have already been identified as having complex needs.

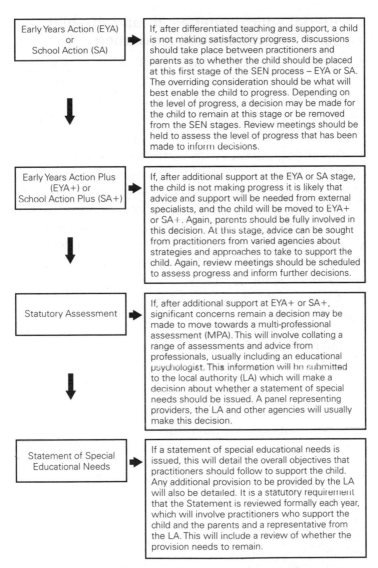

Figure 2.1 An Overview of the SEN Process

Special educational needs and disability discrimination legislation

To tackle discrimination the Disability Discrimination Act was introduced in 1995. It is based on the key principle that disabled people should have the same opportunities as non-disabled people (Kinrade 2003), but disappointingly education was excluded from the initial legislation. In September 2002 additional elements were introduced to the principal legislation, under the Special Educational Needs and Disability Act (SENDA 2001). These were implemented under different special educational needs legislation in England and Scotland, but the same anti-discriminatory duties SENDA places on early years and other educational settings apply equally in the different locations (Riddell 2003). The three main parts of this legislation cover:

♦ Disability discrimination duties (preventing discrimination in educational settings on grounds of disability)

♦ Planning duties (placing an expectation on educational settings to plan for improved access to buildings and services); and to

♦ Work alongside existing special educational needs frameworks.

The overarching aim of the disability discrimination legislation is to equalize access to services and opportunities. Special needs frameworks are an important vehicle for ensuring appropriate provision is in place to meet each child's needs (Disabilities Rights Commission 2002).

Defining disability

Under the legislation a disability is defined as a physical or mental impairment that has a substantial (more than minor and going beyond normal differences) long-term (over 12 months) impact. This also applies to children who have had a disability falling within the definition even if it is no longer present (Disability Rights Commission 2002). To be recognized, a disability must affect at least one aspect of mobility, manual dexterity, physical coordination, continence, ability to learn or the ability of a person to perceive risk or danger (ACE Bulletin 2003). Physical, sensory, learning and recognized mental health disabilities fall within the definition. Medical and progressive conditions, such as epilepsy, diabetes, cancer and HIV are covered if they impact substantially on the ability to carry out normal day-to-day activities (Kinrade 2003). (Further details on this area and how early years settings can meet the needs of children with medical conditions are provided by Dewis (2007).) Emotional and behavioural difficulties are not normally covered, unless they are a result of underlying physical or mental impairment or a mental illness that is diagnosed and well recognized by medical professionals, such as attention deficit or hyperactivity disorder (ACE Bulletin 2003) and this is discussed by Kay (2007). For children with emotional or behavioural difficulties that are not attributed to a recognized medical condition the definition of disability in the legislation would not apply. To meet these needs the special needs framework sets out expectations of early years settings and schools to respond in a graduated way to the needs of each child, and where necessary to call on the support of other agencies (Department for Education and Skills 2001). The legislation excludes conditions such as short-sightedness (which can be corrected with spectacles), broken limbs (as they heal within 12 months), hay fever (seasonal), personality disorders (not clearly defined by medical opinion) and substance or alcohol addiction or dependency (Disability Rights Commission 2002). Criticisms have been made of the definition on the grounds that non-disabled people wrote it and it does not cover all disabilities that may still impact on children.

Defining discrimination

Within the legislation discrimination is defined as 'offering less favourable treatment because a child has a disability' (Kinrade 2003) and applies to actual or prospective pupils in actions relating to school admissions, exclusions, the education setting and related services (e.g. the curriculum, homework, meals, school trips, school and sports facilities) (ACE Bulletin 2003). Discrimination can fall into two areas: treating a disabled pupil (or prospective pupil) less favourably; or failing to take reasonable steps to ensure that actual or prospective pupils are not placed at a substantial disadvantage in comparison to non-disabled pupils (Disability Rights Commission 2002). To decide if discrimination has taken place and if the action taken is justified schools need to ask:

♦ Is the less favourable treatment for a reason that is related to the child's disability?

♦ Is it less favourable treatment that a child without the disability would receive?

♦ Is it less favourable treatment that can be justified?

Within the Act less favourable treatment may be justified if it is related to selection (e.g. admissions criteria); if the child's behaviour is likely to have a serious disruptive influence on other children or the workings of the early years setting or school (Riddell 2003).

Activity

Examples of unjustifiable and justifiable discrimination under the legislation are provided in actual case studies reported by the Disability Rights Commission (2002) but it can be difficult to know at what point actions may become acceptable. Read the following two examples and decide if the actions of the setting would be seen as discrimination under the legislation:

Case study 1

A father is told that his son, who has epilepsy, cannot be admitted to the primary school unless he stops having fits.

> ## Case study 2
>
> A school receives complaints from shopkeepers about the rowdy behaviour of a group of pupils on their way to school. In response to their behaviour it bans the pupils in question from a school visit. One of the pupils has a hearing impairment.

In effect, in the first case study the school is placing conditions on the boy's admission because he might have fits, and not in relation to entry criteria that apply equally to all children. The reason for less favourable treatment relates to the boy's disability and is not acceptable.

In the second case study, the disruptive behaviour is not directly related to the pupil's impairment. Although the ban may be less favourable treatment, it is not related to the pupil's disability and is acceptable.

Preventing discrimination

To prevent discrimination the Act requires the responsible bodies of early years settings and schools (governing bodies in maintained schools in England and the education authority where they manage schools in Scotland) to make reasonable adjustments to avoid disadvantaging children with disabilities in terms of inconvenience, indignity or discomfort. But schools are not currently expected to provide auxiliary aids to assist children (although it is likely that these will be required under existing special needs frameworks) or to make physical adjustments (Riddell 2003), although there are requirements on schools to draw up plans for increasing physical accessibility over time.

If schools act in a way contrary to these requirements parents can complain to schools, local authorities or the Disability Rights Commission. If this does not lead to a satisfactory resolution, cases against the responsible body can also be referred by the pupil (provided they have a general understanding of the issues) or parents to the Special Educational Needs and Disability Tribunal (SENDIST) in England or the Sheriff's court in Scotland. In Wales, Special Educational Needs tribunals started hearing cases from September 2003 and additional duties have been implemented to increase accessibility to this form of redress (Mackenzie 2003).

Concerns have been raised about whether the new legislation acts as a basis for 'political correctness' or in some way could be used to condone irresponsible and inappropriate behaviour on the part of children (Bunt 2001). This is clearly not the case. The purpose of the legislation is about achieving a balance between facilitating access for all and maintaining standards. The legislation shows awareness that children with disabilities or special educational needs have complex needs and face exceptional pressures (Cox 2003). To assist these children and their families the Act places an emphasis on the need to ensure that they receive appropriate support, that resources are used efficiently and that parental concerns are addressed (Henshaw 2003). Evidence of this is provided from appeals figures, which show that in 2002/03 there were 3,772 appeals in relation to special needs and 104 for disability discrimination through SENDIST (Special Educational Needs and Disability Tribunal 2003). More positively there has recently been a reduction in the number of appeals related to special needs (3,637 in 2003/04 and 3,513 in 2004/05), similar to the number in 2001/02. In relation to disability discrimination the number of complaints has remained consistent (108 in 2003/04 and 106 in 2004/05). In this category though a number of claims have been received under the category *Ability to Learn*, which includes dyslexia and autistic spectrum disorders as disabilities, and highlights the broad definition of disability. The percentage of appeals that have been upheld has also remained consistent over the past two years (Special Educational Needs and Disability Tribunal 2005). It is not possible to read too much into these figures but the fact that they are either decreasing or remaining constant, even with the broad definition of disability, could suggest that settings are becoming more skilled in inclusion.

The legislation clearly places expectations on settings to provide appropriate services for children with disabilities and special needs, but it also presents opportunities for practitioners to respond to the needs of children with disabilities by developing high-quality and integrated services. For some children the constraints of a National Curriculum can be problematic. Early years practitioners need to reflect on the approaches that best meet the needs of children, whilst taking account of policy expectations (Mackay 2002). To achieve this, a thorough assessment, carried out in partnership with children and their parents will gain a description of current skills and match these with the curriculum to ensure optimum progress (DfES 2001a, Porter 2002). Opportunities for parents to share information and for this to be recorded accurately, through admission forms, at meetings and in consultation with multi-agency practitioners, will help to ensure effective communication and necessary reasonable adjustments are made to meet the needs of each child. Meeting the requirements of the legislation for children with disabilities is likely to enhance the quality of teaching and learning for non-disabled pupils (Bunt 2001). Cox (2003) highlights the importance of access to skilled practitioners from multiple agencies to promote access to services and opportunities for children with disabilities. Information about transport to appointments, access to auxiliary aids, who to contact for advice and in ensuring steps are taken to ensure any potential language barriers are overcome are examples of issues that need to be addressed to ensure the needs of children and families are met. The challenges of the legislation need to be seen as presenting opportunities for practitioners to create settings that offer integrated services and enable each individual to reach their potential.

The Children Act (2004)

The Children Act (2004) resulted from the comments on the Green Paper *Every Child Matters* (HM Treasury 2003), which was launched by 13 government departments and set out the government's agenda for bringing about change and improvement to child and family services on an unprecedented scale (Waterman and Fowler 2004). A core component of the Green Paper was to set out five outcomes for children that all children's services would work to secure:

- Be healthy
- Stay safe
- Enjoy and achieve
- Make a positive contribution
- Achieve economic well-being

In the subsequent Children Act (2004), which was produced after limited consultation, the five outcomes for improving the health and well-being of children appeared in *legal language* as:

- Physical and mental health and emotional well-being
- Protection from harm and neglect
- Education, training and recreation
- The contribution made by them (children and young people) to society
- Social and economic well-being.

Activity

Compare the outcomes that were listed in *Every Child Matters* with those in the Children Act.

1. Is there a clear link between the two sets of outcomes?

2. What does the difference in wording mean for service providers and how might this benefit children and young people?

> 3. Which of the five outcomes may be relevant to your role as a SENCO?

The two sets of outcomes are clearly linked. The main difference in the wording between the first and second set is that the second, in many respects, is more measurable (as far as this is possible). This is important as the legislation often sets out expectations (i.e. in terms of time limits, through the allocation of duties or detailing procedures) or expected outcomes, which are usually in terms of minimum requirements (i.e. the Children's Commissioner must consult children). For SENCOs it is likely that at some point all of the five outcomes may be relevant to their work. This may not appear to be explicit but all settings will be expected to show regard for the outcomes and consequently they will apply to children with a special need. For some, such as protection from harm and neglect, settings will need to ensure that they have policies and procedures in place at all times for all children. For others, such as education, training and recreation, they may be covered through the curriculum or with support from other agencies. It is also likely that over time, as precedents (when a specific point of law is tested in court and a ruling made to clarify the limits of the point and how this applies in practice) are established, more detailed guidance and expectations that relate to special needs and the SENCO will be issued.

A range of areas covered by the Children Act (2004) will be applicable to a range of education and care establishments, but some of the changes imposed by the legislation may impact more directly on early years settings. For example:

♦ The establishment of a Children's Commissioner who will expect all those working with children to take account of their views and interests. (With the appointment of the Commissioner for England, there is now a commissioner in each country of the United Kingdom.)

♦ In carrying out his role, the Commissioner will take account of the five outcomes for improving the well-being of all children and the United Nations Commission for the Rights of Children (UNCRC), which states minimum levels of provision, protection and participation for all children.

♦ An expectation that private, voluntary and public bodies cooperate to safeguard and promote the welfare of children, including the sharing of information.

♦ Each Children's Services Authority (a partnership body in each local area, including representatives from educational settings) will be required to establish a Local Safeguarding Children Board (LSCB) that will ensure there are effective local policies and procedures in place in each agency to safeguard and promote the welfare of children (DfES 2006). These replaced the non-statutory Area Child Protection Committees (ACPCs) that previously operated in each area.

♦ For looked-after children the local authority (as the *corporate parent*) must consider educational implications when making decisions about care arrangements. This duty does not extend to school governing bodies, but there will clearly need to be effective communication between early years settings and the authority for any looked-after child.

♦ There is now a statutory requirement for local authorities to ensure that the views and wishes of children, consistent with the child's age and level of understanding, are considered when making decisions about service provision.

Conclusion

This chapter has outlined a range of legislation that applies to early years settings in relation to providing for children with special needs and disabilities. Legislation can often seem daunting and as simply placing expectations on settings, but this is clearly not the case. The points outlined show how ongoing legislative changes, although they may be difficult to keep up to date with, are an important vehicle for establishing entitlements for children with SENs or disabilities and in achieving equality for all children in terms of access to settings and in the provision of appropriate care and education. It is also clear with the introduction of the Children Act (2004) that significant emphasis is being placed on the expectation of services to work in partnership, and this is likely to continue for the foreseeable future and will involve the continued development of child and family services.

3

Working with Parents

Introduction

Working with parents and developing positive and effective relationships is important for all children. For parents who have a child with a special need or disability this is particularly important, as they may be unfamiliar with processes and approaches that are utilized to support children. There can also be a view that the best way to support a child is through one-to-one work with an additional practitioner, but this may not necessarily be the case. Therefore, for parents to know that their child has access to appropriate provision and is well supported, it is vital that there is clear communication. All practitioners in the setting need to take responsibility for establishing these relationships and this chapter provides information on how this can be achieved. There is also a number of activities that will promote reflection on factors that impact on the quality of such relationships, and come with suggestions that can be implemented to achieve successful communication.

Creating a positive impression

Understandably, parents want the best for their child and will have high expectations for them. They take significant responsibility for providing for their child and this is usually unproblematic. This may not be the case though when children with a special educational need start to attend an early years setting or school. Clearly, working with parents can be challenging but it is also vital. Read the following case study and then respond to the discussion points. If possible, it is often helpful to discuss your responses with a peer or colleague as this will help you to relate this to practice and reflect on the approaches that you might take.

Case Study

Mr Brookes brings his son, Andrew, into the nursery. In two terms Andrew will start reception class. As the school has a foundation unit the transition shouldn't be an issue as the staff plan and work closely together and many of the activities are delivered in groups that contain nursery and reception-aged children. Andrew and Mr Brookes start to play with some Lego and before long other children have joined them and Andrew starts to explore other activities with some of the children that he has been playing with.

Mr Brookes approaches one of the practitioners and says he wants to see the SENCO before he leaves to 'make sure that there are no problems

---

this time'. Paul, one of the setting managers, tells Mr Brookes that 'the SENCO is busy and will only see people with an appointment, so before you leave it would be best to ask the secretary to make an appointment'. Mr Brookes is not happy with this and demands to see whoever is in charge. Paul explains to Mr Brookes that he is in charge and that he is following the unit policy. At that point Paul explains he is busy and goes to work with a group of children. Mr Brookes leaves, but he is clearly not happy with the situation and spends the rest of the day thinking about how Andrew is doing and the impression he has created.

♦ Why might Andrew's dad have acted in the way he did?

♦ How could this problem have been prevented?

♦ As a practitioner, how would you have acted in this situation?

It is clear from the scenario that this is not the first setting that Andrew has attended and it also seems likely that problems may have occurred previously. If this is the case it is understandable that Mr Brookes was anxious and although he might not have dealt with it in the most appropriate way he was clearly showing concern for his son. Similarly, Paul, the manager, perhaps in response to the initial demands of Mr Brookes, did not handle the situation particularly well. Even though he had to go and work with a group of children, there were other approaches he could have taken or, at least, he could have found a few minutes to listen to Mr Brookes' initial concerns and made a firm time to see him again either later that day or soon afterwards.

When special needs are mentioned it is not particularly unusual for people who work with families to be able to recount stories of difficulties that have occurred in relationships. These may be similar to the above scenario or problems may have arisen in meetings or in communication involving other agencies. To stay with the above scenario, it is fair to say that it may not have been totally preventable but some better planned actions, before Andrew started at the setting, and a more receptive response on the day would have helped. So many problems, such as the one described above, could be prevented if simple procedures and sensitive communication were employed right from the start. Possible approaches could have been:

 ◆ Ensure that relevant information is collected from each family before their child starts and make time to read and respond to any specific points that may impact on a child starting

◆ Where possible undertake a home visit prior to the child starting or organize opportunities for the child to attend the setting prior to starting and ensure that, as part of this, time is included for parents and practitioners to talk

◆ If a child has attended a previous setting, make contact with them to ensure that relevant information and records are passed on to help make the transition as smooth as possible

♦ Provide clear written information about the setting that details who is who, and set out clearly how practitioners in the setting can be contacted (this can also then be referred to once a child has started)

♦ Allocate to each child a key worker, who ideally is available when a child first starts to greet the family and be able to spend some time with them to answer any initial questions or make a note of issues to follow up on

♦ Be open and responsive to parents. Of course there will be times when you are busy and not able to talk but this can be said politely and you can take a contact number and telephone a parent or arrange to meet them soon afterwards.

Developing effective family partnerships

Working with parents requires a considerable investment of time and effort. So it is valid to ask if this is necessary and likely to be productive. It is clear that both the home and the setting contribute significantly to the development of the child (Sylva *et al.* 2004). Some aspects of this may be shared but others are likely to be mainly provided by either home or the setting. Based on this it is clearly beneficial for home and the setting to work together, so the maximum benefit can be derived for the child (Unwin 2005). Bruce (1997) describes this approach as interactionist, where the sharing and exchange of information and knowledge between home and the setting helps to secure the best outcome for the child. This is supported by a range of studies that have shown the benefits that can come from effective partnership working, including raised achievement, increased attendance, and a positive attitude to learning and reduced behaviour problems (Curtis 1998, Chapoudy *et al.* 2001).

This is important for all children but for any child new to a setting and who has a special educational need, there are many potential benefits of establishing an effective and mutually supportive relationship with the family. The transition into a setting can be a challenging time and practitioners need to provide support and reassurance to both parents and children at this time (Kraft-Sayre and Pianta 2000). To achieve this, practitioners and the SENCO need to work together. The SENCO may take responsibility for providing written information about the policies and procedures of the setting to support children with special needs and their family. Practitioners, who will be in day-to-day contact with children and parents, have a vital role in responding to questions, informing parents of progress or concerns and, when necessary, passing information to the SENCO. When practitioners and SENCO work together in this way it is likely that any concerns that parents have will be addressed early, that parents will feel involved in their child's education and that the child will be effectively supported.

For any partnership to be successful it is important to be aware of how the setting of policies and procedures will influence the relationship. As a practitioner who will be seen by a parent as part of the setting, you are in a position of power. Not in the sense that you will dominate the relationship, but because you know your setting, will have developed relationships with colleagues, are aware of the policies and procedures of the setting and are likely to have a broad knowledge of the special needs process. To help equalize this relationship, there are a number of steps that settings can take. Parents should be able to raise issues, ask questions and express views about impending decisions (Whalley 2001), which will help to redress the power differential by showing that decision-making is a consultative process rather than something that is imposed on families (Greenman 2001). This also recognizes the place of parents as their child's primary educator, which is emphasized in the early years curriculum (QCA/DFEE 2000).

In addition, the approach taken by practitioners can have a significant impact on the quality of partnerships that are developed. This does not mean that practitioners need to go to special lengths or alter their practice solely based on the fact that a child has a special need. There are though a number of things that practitioners can do to support and respond to questions or concerns that parents may have. Families have emphasized the importance they attach to practitioners taking time to listen and respond attentively (Adams and Christenson 2000).

Discussion

Think back to the last case study, where Mr Brookes was left feeling frustrated and anxious after the breakdown in communication with Paul, one of the setting managers.

♦ Identify what difficulties occurred that led to the breakdown in communication.
♦ Draw up an action plan that details what you would do to try and maintain positive communication if you found yourself in this situation.

A key guiding principle in maintaining effective communication is that it has to be acknowledged that it is a two-way process. This highlights the importance of ensuring that each party is able to express their views and needs to be prepared to listen to the other. When thinking about how you could respond to this kind of scenario, which is not particularly unusual, you may have thought about it in two different ways: the principles that would guide your response and the actual interaction. Principles that help to establish and maintain effective communication include:

♦ Being respectful towards each other

♦ Allowing each party to express their view without interruption

♦ Recognizing, and if appropriate acknowledging, the unique perspective that a parent brings of their child

♦ Taking an individualized approach to each family

♦ Offering honest responses in a calm and supportive way.

If there has been a previous difficulty, it will often be better to acknowledge this and be open about the need to re-establish effective communication. As well as being important for parents it is also important for children as they may attribute the cause of poor interactions to something they have done (Lawson 2003).

♦ Be positive

♦ Listen attentively

♦ Utilize informal as well as formal opportunities for communication

♦ Involve parents in decision-making.

It is easy to overlook informal opportunities for communicating with families, but they can be extremely helpful in developing effective relationships. Hilliard *et al.* (2001) state that actually taking time to ask parents if there is anything you can do for them can lead to a more open relationship and provide information that enables practitioners to respond to actual rather than perceived needs. Small gestures, such as a personal greeting, taking time to follow up on an earlier conversation or asking for a parent's opinion on an issue are all examples of how practitioners can show respect and openness. This communicates to parents that how they are feeling matters, their input is valued and they are respected.

Informal exchanges are also valuable in building a rapport, and can provide opportunities to learn more about the family culture, composition and interests (Jordan *et al.* 1998), which is particularly important around the time a child starts in a setting.

Parents like to know how their child is progressing when they start nursery or school, and take an active role in their learning and development. Many children will take great delight in sharing their daily experiences with their family. For some children though they may be less reluctant or less able to do this. This could be the case for some children because of a special educational need they may have, such as a communication, learning or developmental difficulty. Practitioners need to be alert to this possibility, either through the knowledge of the child or, as discussed above, through their informal interactions with families. Eldridge (2001) suggests that practitioners can still ensure that families feel involved and able to make a contribution through using informal communication. This can include approaches such as: sending a short note home to highlight how well a child has completed an activity; providing an overview of how they played happily as part of a group; a reminder about an upcoming event; or details about things a child needs to bring for a trip later in the week. Similarly, the same strategy is a useful way for involving the family in supporting their child's learning. So a note may ask the family to take some time practising a counting song, incorporating activities into play that involve use of motor skills, such as playing with Lego or playing games that involve turn taking. As well as facilitating communication this is a way of providing information for parents, which is important for them to be able to support their child (Stewart et al. 2006).

These approaches may seem very simple but can make a significant difference to a child and their family in ensuring they feel involved and that their child is integrated along with other children. Read the case study below. How could the approaches described have made a real difference to how included Kathy and Elizabeth felt?

Case study

Kathy had specially finished work early to collect her daughter, Elizabeth, from school as she wanted to make sure that she had all the information for the class visit the next day. She checked with Sarah, Elizabeth's key worker that all the details for the visit were on the letter that had been sent to parents the week before. Sarah reassured her that all the arrangements were as stated in the letter.

The next morning Elizabeth told her mum she did not want to wear her school uniform because the other children would be wearing their other clothes. Elizabeth wanted to wear her new pink trousers and T-shirt. Kathy explained to Elizabeth that she had to still wear her school clothes as although it was a day out she was going with the school. Elizabeth continued to say that the other children were not wearing their school clothes but Kathy, thinking that children would have to wear their uniform so they were easily identified, insisted that she put her uniform on as usual. When Elizabeth was ready her mum gave her a purse with some money in to spend during the day but she said that they were not allowed to have their own money.

When they arrived at school Kathy was surprised to see that none of the other children had their

---

school uniform on. Elizabeth had been correct, she was able to wear her own clothes but her mum thought that she had not understood as the information as not on the letter. They both went into the classroom and Kathy explained to Sarah what had happened. Luckily Elizabeth had some of her own clothes at school and was able to change.

Again, Kathy explained that she wanted to give Elizabeth some money before leaving home but Elizabeth had told her that the children were not allowed to have their own money. Sarah explained that they had told the children the day before that they could bring some money but it had to be in a wallet and the adult with their group would look after it.

As her mum took Elizabeth into school and had a chance to speak with one of the practitioners the problems were resolved. This situation highlights how helpful it would have been if this information had been clearly communicated to families as this would have prevented the misunderstanding occurring and would have provided an opportunity for the family to talk about the plans together to ensure that they were clear.

The role of key workers in promoting inclusion

When a child starts at a new setting, such as a nursery or reception class, they are likely to come into contact with a group of practitioners. For a child with a SEN, and their family, this is likely to lead to contact with an even larger group of people. As well as practitioners within the learning environment, there may be contact with other staff who have responsibility for special needs and representatives from outside agencies, such as education, health and social care. A key-worker system, where one person takes a coordinating and supportive role for the child and family can be very beneficial in supporting the transition into the setting and ensuring that parents are both informed and involved in decisions related to their child. In addition to benefitting parents, it is also likely that practitioners will have a variety of skills and strengths to meet the increasing expectations of early years settings (Rolfe *et al.* 2003). This offers opportunities, in discussion and agreement with individual practitioners, to allocate key workers to children and families that have skills and knowledge around the child's special need and also has the potential to promote reflection and support their ongoing continuing professional development (Castle 1996). This approach can also be effective in sharing the time demands of communicating with parents, as it is very difficult for one person to have this responsibility for a large group of children. Cole (2005) found that in school settings approximately a third do not seek to work in partnership with parents, although further detail is not provided. Rather than see this as a failing, it may be more of a reflection on time demands on SENCOs and could reinforce the need for a key-worker system to share the demands of communicating with large numbers of parents.

Given the significant developments that have taken place in SEN policy and the emphasis on early intervention and effective provision for children across the policy agenda, it is likely that there will be a continued expectation for SENCOs to take a leading role in providing for children with SEN (e.g. DfES 2001a, HM Treasury 2003, DfES 2004b). This is likely to lead to newcomers, from different agencies, coming together to support children and families. This needs to be seen positively and efforts made to create a sense of identity among practitioners, to promote development of new partnerships, encourage engagement and provide opportunities to learn from each other (Wenger 1998). In turn this will enable key workers to provide effective support for children and to ensure parents are involved and informed. Layton (2005) argues that SENCOs, who have a range of knowledge and skills, need 'to create communities of practice committed to promoting the inclusion of all learners' (p. 57) within their setting. This approach is seen as encompassing three elements:

♦ The domain of knowledge related to supporting children with diverse needs

♦ A group of practitioners who care about the knowledge

♦ Shared practice that is developing is used to develop a culture that is inclusive to all children.

Layton (2005) gives further justification for the importance of inclusion to wider society. The social aim of including all individuals within society, however diverse the abilities, is central to achieving an integrated society. This will only happen though when there is increased understanding of how each individual can be supported and practitioners within the early years sector, with support from SENCOs, have a vital role in starting to contribute to greater inclusion of each individual within society. This may seem a far-reaching aim but, as Layton (2005) identified, there are many tasks that SENCOs are already engaged in that could help to contribute to the aim of inclusion by creating a community of practice, which include:

♦ Listening to colleagues

♦ Good teamwork between the SENCO and other practitioners

♦ Staff believing the SENCO has expertise in SEN

♦ Whole-setting involvement in provision for children with SENs

♦ A positive attitude from all staff to SEN.

For SENCOs to achieve this though it will be vital that they are fully supported in their role and this support will need to come from different channels. Setting managers need to ensure that SENCOs are included in relevant discussions and decision-making forums where changes and developments are likely to impact on children with special needs, as this has a positive impact on creating an inclusive setting (Cole 2005). There will also need to be a commitment to ongoing professional development for all practitioners within a setting, and a more coordinated approach to offering training for management teams (e.g. SENCO, management team, governing body) (Layton 2005).

For these changes to be most effective an integrated approach to effective provision for children with special educational needs across professional boundaries will be needed, supported by local and national policy and practice developments.

Conclusion

A key message from this chapter is that, to develop effective and positive relationships with parents, two-way communication is vital. Practitioners need to remain aware that they come to relationships with parents with a vast amount of knowledge about how a setting works, the staff team and an understanding of procedures. In contrast, parents may not know the setting, it could be their first experience with an early years setting and they are likely to have varying levels of awareness about any potential special need. To establish a good relationship, practitioners can make a significant contribution to providing information and supporting parents by adopting strategies outlined in this chapter. One final point to remember is that often, as a practitioner, your actions can make a significant difference to families. This may often not be evidenced to practitioners but this does not mean it is not valued.

4

Promoting Inclusion and Children's Participation

Introduction

Over recent years awareness has increased about the importance of involving children in decision-making where the outcomes will have an impact on them. Often there is a desire to include children fully in decision-making processes but practitioners can find this challenging. There can be a variety of reasons behind this, including how to communicate and involve young children, finding time and devising approaches that enable children to be included in a meaningful way. This chapter will discuss the importance of consulting young children and how this can have a positive impact on promoting emotional well-being and social relationships. Throughout the chapter approaches that can be applied in practice to achieve meaningful participation are suggested. Although the focus of this book is about ensuring that there is an organized and high-quality approach to the appropriate provision for children with a SEN, many of the strategies discussed in this chapter apply to all children.

What does inclusion and participation involve?

Activity

Record your responses to each of the following questions.

1. What is inclusion?

2. What do you see as the benefits of creating an inclusive setting?

3. What do you see as the challenges of creating an inclusive setting?

4. If a setting has a negative attitude to inclusion how is this likely to impact on families and children?

5. If a setting has a positive attitude to inclusion how is this likely to impact on families and children?

The introduction of the 2001 SENCOP brought with it a change in the language applied to special needs. The code signalled an expectation that wherever possible children with a special need or disability should be educated in mainstream settings (Jones 2004). To create an inclusive environment it is necessary to think about integration and participation. If this is not done, a child with an SEN might be included in terms of being there but not in terms of feeling integrated or being given the opportunity to participate. A key strategy to avoid this and create an environment where all children are able to reach their potential is a commitment to increasing the level of children's participation. Jones (2004) states that an important element of this is creating an environment and team that:

♦ Celebrates and appreciates differences rather than categorizes and separates

♦ Sees diversity as ordinary

♦ Recognizes and values the principle of learning together

♦ Creates an environment where children have friends regardless of individual differences

♦ Has mutual respect and regard for others.

Children's right to participation

The United Nations Convention on the Rights of the Child (UNCRC), which was adopted in 1989, has the key principles of listening to the child's opinion, acting in their best interest and preventing discrimination at its heart. In practice this means that practitioners need to consider approaches that ensure that children are able to participate in decisions, are protected from harm and have access to appropriate provision. This is clearly expressed in Article 12, which:

♦ states parties shall assure the child who is capable of forming his or her own views the right to express those views freely in all matters affecting the child, the views of the child being given due weight in accordance with the age and maturity of the child.

♦ states for this purpose, the child shall in particular be provided the opportunity to be heard in any judicial and administrative procedures affecting the child, either directly or through a representative or an appropriate body, in a manner consistent with the procedural rules of national law (UNICEF 1989).

In effect, this is stating that all children need to be given the opportunity to know what decisions are being made and have the opportunity, in a way that takes account of their level of development, to express their view (DfES 2001a). To achieve this, the responsibility for involving the child does not need to rest solely with an early years setting. This presents opportunities to work in partnership with the family so that opinions expressed by the child at home are welcomed and encouraged and can feed into the decision-making process.

Reflection

Think about either developments you have implemented or seen being implemented in your setting, or changes that have occurred based on external policies (e.g. introducing a new curriculum) or an externally controlled event (e.g. inspection). For example, changing a working practice or putting together an information pack about a setting.

> ◆ Who would you identify as the main stakeholders affected by the development or change?
> ◆ Is there any evidence that each group of stakeholders were consulted (this could have happened as part of an earlier stage) and their views taken account of?
> ◆ Is there any evidence, either directly or indirectly from each group, that the change was in their best interest?

It is likely that children were one of the key stake-holding groups that you identified. It is also likely that the level of consultation involving children was not as good as it could have been. An example of this is evident in the government's plans for developing extended schools. The proposal is to establish a range of services within schools that will provide education and care between the hours of 8am and 6pm throughout the year. Many children already attend breakfast or after-school clubs that extend their day but these proposals signal a significant development and expansion of this provision. There is an assumption here that children and their families will be happy with this, when in fact there is no evidence that children have been consulted. A research study by Smith and Barker (2000) identified that although many children enjoyed attending after-school provision the level of enjoyment decreased with age. Another significant finding was that over three quarters of children were there because their parents were working. In addition, one of the activities most enjoyed by children was spending time with their families, which is likely to reduce significantly if these proposals are implemented (Smith and Barker 2001).

This raises questions about what significance this has for child participation in early years settings. Simply, practitioners need to see any effort to increase the participation level of children as a welcome and positive development in practice. At all levels of policy development and service provision, as illustrated above, there is evidence of poor levels of consultation and involvement of children, who are often the key recipients of services. Therefore, where there is evidence of developments and initiatives to increase participation in individual settings this is extremely positive and practitioners need to concentrate on successes rather than be overly concerned with what is still to be achieved.

Before any approach to increase participation is implemented it is important to think about what the purpose is. If the aim is to obtain feedback on how much a child has enjoyed a new activity it may take a very informal approach. If the aim is to gain a clear overview of a child's perspective on activities on their IEP it will be useful to have this recorded in some way. The case study below highlights how this can still be done in a way that utilizes many of the strategies discussed in this chapter and shows it is not necessary to rely on formal documents to convey the child's view. It is also important to be clear that gaining the child's view on targets, and the strategies that have been used to achieve them, is as important as assessments that aim to measure progress that has been made.

Case study

Darren, who has difficulty communicating, had been at the nursery for four months. When he first started, the setting had worked in partnership with his parents and the speech and language therapist to implement an IEP based on the advice received. Julie, his key worker, wanted to evaluate these approaches and gain Darren's perspective on what he enjoyed, where he had progressed and his general view of nursery.

To make this assessment Julie set aside time to work with Darren. Rather than ask him a whole list of questions, which he may have difficulty understanding and responding to, she decided to play alongside him. She initially approached Darren and asked if he would like to play. He said yes and she encouraged him to choose an activity. He wanted to paint so they decided to do a picture together. She held back to give Darren a chance to initiate the activity. He led the way to the creative area, and was able to find the materials independently and prepared the water and brushes. He asked Julie what colours she wanted and reminded her of the need to wear an apron by picking one up and giving it to her. When they were painting Julie used the opportunity to ask Darren to paint things he enjoyed doing at nursery. Through talking together she also found out that Darren did not like being asked questions.

During the rest of the session she observed Darren playing with other children, taking part in a wide range of activities, and she was surprised to note how much he enjoyed singing. She also noticed that the children that Darren played with the most were not part of the group he sat with. This information, notes from her observations and the paintings of the things that Darren enjoyed and disliked, along with other assessments completed, were all presented and discussed at his review meeting. They enabled a good assessment to be made of his progress and gave a good basis for the establishment of new targets. After the meeting Julie worked with the speech and language therapist who advised on different strategies, which utilized activities that Darren enjoyed, to achieve these targets. It was also decided, in discussion with Darren and his mum, that he would work in a group that had three children he enjoyed playing with and felt comfortable talking to.

Effective practice to promote participation

Consulting children can be time-consuming and may present challenges to practitioners. It should not be seen though as separate from learning but, rather, as part of it. The Curriculum Guidance (QCA/DfES 2000) and Birth to Three Matters (SureStart 2003) both emphasize the need for children to develop skills that will enable them to participate. For young children this includes:

♦ Developing social confidence, competence and an increasing level of independence

♦ Demonstrating preferences and making choices about activities

♦ Having opportunities to explore and develop a positive attitude to change

♦ Feeling included, secure and valued.

Activity

Imagine you have been asked to produce an information guide for practitioners in the Foundation Stage to embed these strategies. The aim of the guide is to incorporate activities into the curriculum that are stimulating, challenging and likely to be enjoyed by the children. What approaches and suggestions would you include to ensure that all children were able to benefit?

Varied approaches can be embedded in activities and working practices to increase the participation of children, and these are discussed throughout the chapter. Additional guidance from the DfES (2001c) identifies a range of principles that are important for practitioners and settings to ensure children's participation is part of day-to-day working, which include:

♦ Everyone in the setting needs to take responsibility and be committed to the challenges of increasing child participation.

♦ There must be respect for the interests of all partners in decision-making processes.

- Children need opportunities to learn about the importance of participating and becoming actively involved.

- Settings need to be warm, welcoming and open to children and families.

Activity

It can be difficult to explain the concept of rights to young children. To assist this, there are many resources available to help practitioners explain to children why their opinions are important and why they need to behave respectfully to others. The UNICEF UK website has a wide range of information that can assist practitioners and various resources that can be incorporated into teaching plans.

1. Spend some time browsing the information and resources on the UNICEF UK website (http://www.unicef.org.uk).

2. There are many other websites that can be useful for providing information and resources. For example, the Children's Commissioner for England, Wales, Northern Ireland and Scotland all have good information. The DfES has a number of research reports that include discussion of strategies to involve children. Article 12 is a website for children and run by children.

3. Create a brief overview of useful information you find, including relevant links.

---

4. Discuss this in a staff meeting or development session and distribute it among practitioners to increase awareness of this important issue.

5. If increasing the involvement of children in decision-making processes is a priority in your setting this discussion could be helpful for agreeing 2–3 key aims and devising an action plan to achieve these within a set time period.

An example of a useful resource from UNICEF UK is the *Children's Little Book of Rights*. This clearly explains to children in primary education what the concept of rights is about. The book uses simple and accessible language to explain each article of the UNCRC (see Figure 4.1). It also explains to children that rights and responsibilities go hand-in-hand (see Figure 4.2). The booklet is a useful teaching resource to show children why their opinion is important and how the way they act impacts on how they and people around them feel. This is important as it provides a context to show how respecting and valuing each other is a key part of forming social relationships and resolving problems in a positive way. This may not all be fully understood by young children but as they progress through the Foundation Stage and Key Stage 1 these issues will be increasingly developed and understood. For pre-literate children the concepts that are developed in Figures 4.1 and 4.2 can be integrated into activities linked to visual representations and discussion (e.g. us and how we relate to others) in addition to relying solely on the printed text.

ARTICLE 15

CHILDREN HAVE THE RIGHT TO MEET TOGETHER AND TO JOIN GROUPS AND ORGANISATIONS, AS LONG AS THIS DOES NOT STOP OTHER PEOPLE FROM ENJOYING THEIR RIGHTS.

ARTICLE 16

CHILDREN HAVE A RIGHT TO PRIVACY. THE LAW SHOULD PROTECT THEM FROM ATTACKS AGAINST THEIR WAY OF LIFE, THEIR GOOD NAME, THEIR FAMILIES AND THEIR HOMES.

ARTICLE 17

CHILDREN HAVE THE RIGHT TO RELIABLE INFORMATION FROM THE MASS MEDIA. TELEVISION, RADIO, AND NEWSPAPERS SHOULD PROVIDE INFORMATION THAT CHILDREN CAN UNDERSTAND, AND SHOULD NOT PROMOTE MATERIALS THAT COULD HARM CHILDREN.

8

9

ARTICLE 18

BOTH PARENTS SHARE RESPONSIBILITY FOR BRINGING UP THEIR CHILDREN, AND SHOULD ALWAYS CONSIDER WHAT IS BEST FOR EACH CHILD. GOVERNMENTS SHOULD HELP PARENTS BY PROVIDING SERVICES TO SUPPORT THEM, ESPECIALLY IF BOTH PARENTS WORK.

ARTICLE 19

GOVERNMENTS SHOULD ENSURE THAT CHILDREN ARE PROPERLY CARED FOR, AND PROTECT THEM FROM VIOLENCE, ABUSE AND NEGLECT BY THEIR PARENTS, OR ANYONE ELSE WHO LOOKS AFTER THEM.

ARTICLE 20

CHILDREN WHO CANNOT BE LOOKED AFTER BY THEIR OWN FAMILY MUST BE LOOKED AFTER PROPERLY, BY PEOPLE WHO RESPECT THEIR RELIGION, CULTURE AND LANGUAGE.

ARTICLE 21

WHEN CHILDREN ARE ADOPTED THE FIRST CONCERN MUST BE WHAT IS BEST FOR THEM. THE SAME RULES SHOULD APPLY WHETHER THE CHILDREN ARE ADOPTED IN THE COUNTRY WHERE THEY WERE BORN, OR IF THEY ARE TAKEN TO LIVE IN ANOTHER COUNTRY.

10

11

Figure 4.1

Figure 4.2 Whose Responsibility (UNICEF UK)

Measuring participation

If a setting wants to know the level of participation that is occurring or has plans to enhance it, it is helpful to know about current practice. This raises the question of how the level of participation can be measured. Hart (1992) suggested that participation could be measured at different levels and to do this, devised the *ladder of participation*. The ladder sets out decisions in a relatively hierarchical way but clearly shows how levels of participation vary from low (e.g. children do what adults suggest they do) to child-initiated, shared decisions with adults. This representation could suggest that the level of participation is relatively static over a range of areas. Another criticism is the idea that the highest level of participation should always be aimed for when differences in levels of participation may occur for valid reasons. For example, the level of participation that could be encouraged among a group of children building a tent will be much higher than expected if an instruction is given by a practitioner to prevent a dangerous situation occurring. In response to this Treseder (1997) devised five levels of participation:

♦ Child-initiated, shared decisions with adults

♦ Child-initiated and directed

♦ Adult-initiated, shared decisions with children

♦ Children assigned but informed

♦ Children consulted and informed.

Unlike Hart, the different levels are not hierarchical but are intended to be seen as equal and each as an exemplar of good practice. For example, where children are *assigned but informed*, adults may decide on an activity but children are involved as they volunteer to participate. Treseder's approach acknowledges that there are different methods, which all have effective elements that can enhance levels of participation.

Both of these approaches offer valuable strategies for measuring levels of participation. In day-to-day practice it is likely that different levels of participation will be both desirable and appropriate and dependent on the situation. The level of participation may also vary within a setting among different practitioners. To take account of this, Figure 4.3 presents another approach to measure, discuss and evaluate levels of participation. Rather than take a linear approach, it may be helpful to see participation as varying both within and between activities and interactions, and when evaluating the level it is important to take account of the context. The model, which is designed to reflect early years practice, offers the opportunity for practitioners to reflect on how levels of participation can be enhanced by looking at the range of descriptions.

Promoting participation

Save the Children have focused on promoting participation among children. O'Malley (2004) produced a report for the organization about the lessons that had been learnt to promote children's participation in international work. Although the report was focused at policy-making level, the factors that contributed to effective participation could clearly be applied to children and adults in early years settings:

♦ Children need to be well-informed

♦ Effective participation takes considerable time

♦ Feedback needs to be given to promote continued participation (even if it is to explain why something cannot happen)

♦ The most potentially marginalized children need to be included

♦ It is important to involve adults as this will help to ensure children are listened to

♦ Partnerships need to be developed to share effective practice.

Child takes the lead and may initiate ideas, decisions are
shared with adults

Child-initiated ideas or choices and support from adults
about what to pursue

Adult-initiated plans or choices, shared decisions with
children about what to pursue

Adult-initiated and child-informed with opportunity
given for feedback

Choices provided by adults and children are able to choose

Children are given the opportunity to express their view
but it does not impact on opportunities for the child

Children take part in events, such as a play it is not explained
to them and they are not asked if they want to participate

Children do what others say they will do and there are no
opportunities for consultation

Figure 4.3 Promoting decision-making and
participation (adapted from Hart (1992))

Miller *et al.* (2005) argue that a key component of listening to children and encouraging participation is creating a positive and welcoming learning environment, as Julie did in the previous case study. When you enter somewhere new you get a sense of how open it is. Young children may not think of it in those terms but they will still get a sense of how happy, included and settled they feel. To be open a setting needs to provide opportunities for all to ask questions, to promote and welcome discussion, and be willing to discuss new ideas and approaches. An important aspect of development for young children is developing a sense of identity (Smith *et al.* 2003). A setting that allows them to make choices, express their opinion, try out new ideas and take managed risks is vital to support this. This does not mean that children should do exactly what they want but they can be supported in understanding different choices and the potential outcome of these. For example, in some settings if it is raining children do not go outside but often adults have to or choose to walk in the rain. It does not need to be any different for children. In the same way that adults will put on a waterproof coat and suitable footwear so can children. In this sense their choice is respected but they will also understand that to stay dry, warm and to protect their day clothes they need to wear appropriate clothing outside. The activity below will be useful in helping you gain an overview of how well the environment supports children's participation, and to identify changes that could support children to make decisions and choices more independently.

Activity

The environment can have a significant impact on the level of participation. Look around your early years setting and make an assessment of how it promotes and restricts participation. If you identify any potential barriers discuss these with another person to identify potential solutions. The following points may help with the assessment:

♦ Are activities accessible to children without the need for adult assistance?
♦ Are resources positioned in areas where they are easy to access?
♦ Is the environment organized in a way that encourages children to utilize all of the space?
♦ Are there spaces for the children to work independently on their own and in groups?
♦ Is there freedom for children to negotiate how they work? For example, if an area attracts too many children are they given the opportunity to resolve this for themselves?
♦ Is there free access to outdoor space?
♦ Are there areas for quiet working, sitting, working on the floor and to engage in creative activities that children can access independently?
♦ Do children have access to suitable clothing and footwear to take part in varied activities inside and outside in different weather conditions?

Strategies to increase children's participation

In addition to the points discussed so far, curriculum documents offer ideas and strategies to ensure that children are listened to and have the opportunity to participate in day-to-day activities and decision-making. In school environments there may also be an opportunity to participate in a school council, giving children the opportunity to express their view and those of their peers on school-related issues. If a school council is in operation, children with a SEN should have the same opportunity to participate. In early years settings, for participation to be effective, open communication is key. To support this, practitioners will need to implement and encourage informal approaches. The following strategies will help to enhance communication and increase children's participation:

♦ Provide opportunities for conversations to occur between adults and children, rather than only requiring children to respond to questions

♦ When children are talking show genuine interest in what they have to say and respect their choice if they choose not to communicate

♦ Create opportunities to promote talk between children and practitioners

♦ Provide opportunities for children to work in different sized groups with others they feel confident with and where they have opportunities to contribute without being interrupted

♦ Use circle time and other approaches to promote self-identity and development of social skills

♦ Utilize observation to gain an insight into what children do and do not enjoy doing

♦ Think about adaptations that can be made to the environment to enable children to choose activities they enjoy and develop independence. For example pictures on the front of storage boxes, large print labels or communication symbols

♦ Take account of any particular difficulty a child may have that could impact on their level of participation and try to think about approaches that overcome these. Advice and support could come from other professionals who work with the child.

Recently there has been an increase in the number of research projects that have utilized methods that promote the participation of children (e.g. Clark 2004). The rationale behind this is that it is recognized that children are the *experts on their lives* and are best placed to tell others their opinions, what is important to them and issues that concern them. Clark (2004) supports the notion of children being the *experts on their lives* and developed participatory methods to increase participation by children known as the Mosaic approach. Although these are designed as research methods they offer the potential for practitioners to gain children's views of what is important to them and what they enjoy by using varied communication tools. The following approaches could be valuable strategies for practitioners to gain an insight into children's experiences:

♦ **Use of cameras**. These could be disposable or digital cameras and they could be given to children to take pictures in the setting of scenes that are important to them. This could include pictures of activities they particularly enjoy or dislike, or areas they like to play in. The pictures could also provide artefacts for children to use in conversations with practitioners to help verbalize their thoughts and feelings.

♦ **Going on a tour of the setting or making a map from materials they have collected on the tour**. Practitioners could accompany a child on the tour or they could be given a portable audio recorder to record their thoughts as they go round. If a practitioner accompanies a child it is almost like a walking interview. The benefit of this approach is that the child chooses where they want to go and discussion with a practitioner should revolve around the child's choice. Similarly, if a child chooses to make a map of the setting the same principles should apply.

♦ **Child conferences**. This is perhaps the most 'formal' approach and is likely to occur with older children. If this method is used it will usually be to gain a group of children's perspectives on their early education setting. Clark (2004) uses questions to find out why children come to nursery, what they enjoy doing while there and things that they find hard. It is likely that during these conferences children will also provide other information about things that are important to them.

In addition to practical approaches, Thomas (2001) discusses the importance of listening to children to promote good communication. He argues that there are a number of reasons why this is important, which are:

♦ because they have a right to be heard,

♦ because it is good for them,

♦ because it leads to better decisions.

He also supports the view that listening to children should be seen as part of everyday practice – not a specialist skill. Early years practitioners do not generally have difficulties communicating with adults and this should be the same with children. Part of the role of a SENCO is to work with practitioners and help them to recognize the skills they already have for working with children. It is likely that they already have a high level of confidence in ensuring that children have opportunities to participate but it may be helpful to increase their awareness of these. To enhance this further though Thomas (2001) identified a number of strategies that children highlighted as leading to good communication that support approaches discussed earlier:

♦ Ensure that there is ample time to communicate with children, and work at a pace that the child is comfortable with and allows them to stay in control.

♦ Allow children time to get to know and trust you and ensure that all communication is open and honest. The key-worker system can support this as it provides a basis for a child to develop a relationship with a person they trust over a sustained period of time.

♦ Give children the choice of when they want to participate in decision-making and allow them time to prepare.

♦ Take a supportive approach to communication and actively encourage children to express their view. Some children may prefer to tell an adult what they think and will feel more comfortable if the adult passes this on, particularly in an unfamiliar environment such as a review meeting.

♦ Allow the child to set the agenda for the communication. This is more likely to encourage the child to speak about issues that are important to them rather than simply respond to questions from adults.

♦ Make it fun. Communicating with children should be fun. What is being discussed is important but this should not stop a fun approach being taken. The more enjoyable the experience is, the more likely children are to participate.

♦ Effective communication involves a level of risk-taking. Sometimes things will not go as planned but children can learn from this and develop an increasing sense of autonomy.

Conclusion

As this chapter has shown, the emphasis on increasing children's participation has increased over recent years. Legislation, codes of practice and policies have all been produced to help achieve this aim. In addition there is a further important consideration – how practitioners in early years settings can help to make increased children's participation a reality. For children to feel valued, included and have the opportunity to fully participate, practitioners need to have a commitment to participation and the skills to achieve this. This chapter has outlined how important it is for practitioners to see this as a day-to-day practice. The strategies and approaches outlined in the chapter, and the skills practitioners already have provide a sound basis for further enhancing levels of participation among children. It is also worth noting that the strategies discussed in this chapter offer the potential to develop high-quality experiences throughout a setting. All children will benefit from being in a setting where practitioners value their opinion and take active steps to find out their views.

Part 2

Putting Things into Practice

The overall aim of Part 2 is to review the processes and procedures that SENCOs are involved in and offer suggestions to support and develop effective practice. To achieve this, the chapters will discuss a range of tasks and roles that a SENCO usually participates in or coordinates (many of which are detailed in the SEN Code of Practice). The chapters offer guidance on reviewing and enhancing the overall management and coordination of special needs. Practitioners, who either want to learn more about the role of the SENCO or already hold the role, need to consider the suggestions in the context of their own setting. The degree to which the suggestions are relevant, practical and possible needs to be appropriate for your own context and the person who knows most about this is you.

5

Special Needs Policy

If you go into any early years setting it is likely that they will have a folder that contains various policies for that setting, covering a broad range of issues. Some of these policies may be the result of national requirements (e.g. through legislative requirements, expectations of the Early Years Directorate of Ofsted, the Local Authority or as part of an organization hierarchy). Among them, there will be a SEN policy; it is a requirement that all maintained and early years settings in receipt of government funding for education have a SEN policy (DfES 2001b). In maintained schools the governing body has the overall responsibility for producing this policy. It is usual though for it to be drafted or amended by practitioners and then presented for discussion to the governors. Just because the policy is there, though, it does not mean that it is fully implemented, informs day-to-day practice or is helpful to practitioners. Similarly, parents and children may not benefit from the implementation of the policy in the way that is intended. The aim of this chapter is to discuss how policies can be developed and implemented in a way that supports practitioners, provides high-quality care for children and informs and involves parents.

Activity

Many examples of SEN policies for early years settings and schools are available on the Internet. Spend some time locating 3–4 examples of these policies and consider the following points:

1. Is it clear what the policy is for and what it is intended to achieve?

2. Do the different sections of the policy fit well with each other? For example, if a stated aim is for children to be consulted do other parts of the policy give some insight into the actual minimum expectations of what this means and how it will be achieved?

3. Is there some evidence of how the policy will (or is intended to) impact on day-to-day practice?

4. Is it evident who the policy will impact on and how this has been communicated to the different groups?

5. Is it clear when the policy will next be reviewed?

6. Look through the different policies that you have collated. Are there similarities between them that show they have been informed by relevant legislation and guidance? This should be the case, as all settings that receive funding will be working within the remit of similar legislative and policy requirements.

Looking at other examples of policy can be a useful starting point for writing a new or updating a current policy. A valid question to ask is, Why it is important to have a written policy? The danger is that policies are written and filed away and the impact they are intended to have does not materialize in practice. This could happen for many reasons. It may be that some policies do not impact on everyday practice and only need to be referred to for specific advice (e.g. to find out entitlement to time off for a special occasion). Sometimes, policies are written that are intended to inform practice but custom and routine continues to be the main influence. This does not necessarily mean that the practice is poor or unacceptable but it does mean that practice is dependent on the presence of the same group of practitioners and it may be that other groups, such as parents, are not fully aware of what is happening.

For SENCOs, the special educational needs policy has the potential to be a valuable resource to both inform and guide practice and ensure that measures are in place to be inclusive and responsive to the needs of all children and their families in an equitable way. Baldock *et al.* state that written policies can help to achieve this in two ways (2005: 9):

◆ The process of composing a written statement can in itself help to clarify ideas that may be shared but not sufficiently articulated, or to uncover disagreements that had not previously surfaced so that these can be resolved.

◆ A written statement is an essential step in communicating the policy to others (even though this is not usually adequate in itself). The others include, of course, those staff who might join the setting for which the policy was created at a later date.

Activity

Locate a copy of the SEN policy for the setting you work in (or one of the policies from the previous activity). Look through the policy and consider the following questions:

1. Is it clear what the overall aims and objectives of the policy are?
2. Does the policy provide a sufficient level of detail to inform practice?
3. Is it clear how parents and children are consulted and involved in decisions and procedures related to special needs?
4. If you needed guidance on an aspect of practice (e.g. reviewing and updating an Individual Education Plan (IEP)) would the policy be helpful?
5. If you were new to the setting and wanted guidance on how you were expected to support a child with SEN and who you could go to for advice, would the policy be useful?

As well as your own responses to these questions it would also be useful to talk to other practitioners to gain their perspective. It may be that there are different views within the setting.

The activity above could be a useful starting point for considering in what ways your current SEN policy is effective and areas where review is needed. One of the challenges, as outlined above, is to ensure that all practitioners within a setting are familiar with it and utilize it to guide their practice. If this does not happen, it could be because practitioners do not see the benefit of referring to the policy or feel ownership of it. To overcome this, the policy needs to be written in a style that both explains its broad objective but also contains information in an accessible way to guide and inform practice. If a SEN policy is to meet the expectations in the activity above it will need to contain information on how the setting responds to a broad range of issues, such as:

◆ Overall aims and objectives of what the policy is intended to achieve

◆ The role and responsibilities of the setting's management team, the SENCO and practitioners who work with children (these will need to be written in the context of your own setting, e.g. the responsibility of teachers and teaching assistants)

◆ How to respond if a child is identified as potentially having a SEN

◆ Information on the different aspects of practice that are covered by the policy (e.g. reviewing and writing IEPs review meetings contact with multi-professionals moving between stages of the Code of Practice, etc.)

◆ Procedures for consulting with children

♦ Working in partnership with parents to ensure they are fully involved in procedures and decision-making

♦ How to respond to complaints

♦ Information that may be specific to your setting (e.g. if there is a specific unit to support children with a specific type of educational need).

These points should not be seen as suggesting that the SEN policy needs to contain specific details on every aspect of practice. This would be neither possible nor helpful. What the policy can do though is offer clear guidance on:

♦ How children with SENs are an integral part of the setting

♦ How to approach partnerships with parents and children

♦ How to promote inclusion and ensure there is a consistent and high-quality response to support each child with special needs.

For example, a policy would not need to set out the exact timings for reviewing IEPs but would give guidance on how frequently a review should be undertaken. The point was made earlier that policies are often written and then confined to a file and very rarely consulted. In the approach outlined above, as well as setting out the broad aims of the setting, the policy will also be useful to practitioners and it is far more likely to be consulted routinely. In this way policies offer the potential to be useful documents for SENCOs by offering unambiguous advice on procedures and practice and by ensuring a consistent approach for all children and for practitioners. To support a setting in drafting an SEN policy, local authorities, other settings and visiting professionals may be able to provide examples of policies that could offer guidance.

The approaches discussed in this chapter have shown how an appropriately drafted and implemented special needs policy has the potential to inform and guide practice. In addition, the regular use of the policy as one of the central points of reference will help to achieve a level of consistency in the approach to practice that will be beneficial to practitioners, children and parents.

6

Individual Education Plans (IEPs)

Introduction

An Individual Education Plan (IEP) should be seen as central to the planning for a child with a SEN. At a simple level it can be seen as a document that lays out the approach to be taken to support an individual child and it is important that they are fully utilized to offer the maximum benefit to each child and their family. This chapter discusses a range of issues around the formulating, implementing and reviewing of IEPs, and the role of the SENCO in supporting their colleagues to in turn fully support each child.

Identifying children with SEN

Every child who is identified as having SEN should have an IEP. The only exception to this is if the needs of children are fully addressed by the differentiated planning that is already in place. If this is the case it is still necessary for records of attainment to show clearly how any child with SEN is progressing and achieving the specified targets. Under the previous Code of Practice, if there was an initial concern about a child they would have been placed on stage one of the Code. The revised Code of Practice (DfES 2001a) reduced the number of stages and now children are either at Early Years Action or Action Plus or School Action or Action Plus. The new code also emphasizes the importance of taking a graduated approach to special needs (DfES 2001b). In practice this means that before a child is identified as having SEN or moved to another stage, a set of planned actions should have been devised, implemented and evaluated to see how the individual child progressed. If this approach is followed it will help to ensure that children who are experiencing a temporary or specific difficulty are given the chance to progress through differentiated planning and appropriate support, without being identified as having SEN. This is particularly important in the early years as, although children may not appear to be progressing, there may be variations in the age at which individual children reach specific milestones (Smith, Cowie and Blades 2003, Sylva *et al.* 2004). A variation should not automatically be seen as problematic – it may simply reflect individual difference. For example, based on knowledge of child development, it will not be surprising if girls achieve reading and writing targets before boys.

If the above process is followed this should mean that only children who actually require some intervention, which is different from that covered by differentiated planning, will need an IEP. There may also be occasions when a group of children have very similar needs and a group IEP can be used in this situation. This is completely acceptable as it is neither necessary nor productive to produce IEPs with identical targets, yet individual records of how well each individual child is progressing towards the targets do need to be maintained.

What is an IEP and what should it contain?

This will vary between settings but DfES guidance (2001d) states that:

♦ An IEP is a planning, teaching and reviewing tool. It will cover what is specific to a child (or group of children) to help them progress.

♦ The IEP should contain a maximum of four targets and should link, as far as possible, with areas from the Foundation Stage or Key Stage One curriculum document.

♦ It should detail what will be taught, how this will be taught and the frequency of this through additional or different activities through the differentiated curriculum.

♦ The IEP should be seen as the structured planning documentation that will be implemented to help achieve the specified targets.

♦ IEPs should be accessible and clear for all practitioners who work with the child.

♦ Where possible the child and parent should be involved in devising the IEP.

♦ If a child has a statement of SEN, the IEP targets and specified teaching strategies should be linked to the overall objectives that are set out in the statement.

♦ When being devised, IEPs need to take account of what is manageable in terms of time and resources for each setting. This will ensure that the specified targets are more likely to be achievable.

♦ IEPs need to be seen as an integral part of the planning for the setting and will therefore be under continual review. In addition a more formal review process will need to be undertaken (this is discussed in more detail below).

Setting IEP targets

A particular challenge when writing IEPs can be in the setting of achievable targets. The best targets will state clearly what is to be achieved and the time it is expected to be achieved in. If a child does not meet a specific target this should not be seen as a failure, but an indication that either the target needs to be revised, more time is needed or alternative teaching strategies or activities may be appropriate. The guidance (DfES 2001d) suggests that it is helpful to think about including SMART targets:

♦ **S**pecific

♦ **M**easurable

♦ **A**chievable

♦ **R**elevant

♦ **T**ime bound

There are a number of commercially produced programmes to assist with writing IEPs. For further information, the BECTA website offers an overview of software for IEP writing and SEN management (see www.becta.org.uk). These generally allow targets to be generated from a range of curriculum areas. They can be beneficial in terms of saving time and identifying manageable steps to assist progression. It is still necessary though for practitioners to make any necessary adaptations and to include a clear level of detail about how the teaching and resources will be organized to enable the targets to be achieved in the context of their setting. A potential shortcoming of this approach to producing IEPs is that they may lead to less involvement of children and parents in drafting the plan. It is also possible that using a programme for drafting IEPs could lead to a more segregated approach to supporting children with SENs and the planning process for other children in the setting or class. Care is needed to avoid this, as it is likely to lead to unmanageable demands on practitioners and reduce the likelihood of targets being achieved.

Reviewing IEPs

The process of reviewing IEPs, to ensure that adequate progress is being made, make necessary revisions and plan for further development is important. In many settings there is often a set regime in operation for the review of IEPs. For example, they might be reviewed three times per year, at approximately termly intervals. Rightly so, there is no set standard approach for reviewing IEPs. The only expectation is that they will be reviewed formally at least twice a year. For some children, this may be adequate. For example, if a child has a specific need where a planned programme of work has been implemented and there is ongoing review and revision. For other children, particularly children in the foundation stage, IEPs may need to be reviewed on a much more regular basis as targets may be very specific and achieved more quickly. This could be as frequently as six times per year. Again, this does not have to involve a specially organized review meeting on every occasion but good practice should ensure, as far as possible, that children and parents are involved in the review process. A review may also lead to one or two targets being changed rather than the whole IEP. In early years settings, parents are often seen most days, which offers regular opportunities for short informal discussions that can contribute to the review and to copies of new plans being discussed and shared. The decision as to when to review an IEP needs to be based on:

♦ Evidence from ongoing assessment, of a target being achieved or difficulty in achieving a target

♦ Feedback from a child or parent in relation to one or more targets

♦ Input from external specialists, such as a speech and language therapist or health visitor

♦ Part of an annual review for a child who has a statement of special educational needs (although the main aspect of this meeting is to review the overall objectives set out in the statement)

♦ A view that a change needs to be made in the stage a child is at in the special needs process (i.e. to move from Early Years Action Plus to Early Years Action)

♦ The timing between past reviews. If there is evidence from past reviews that the time taken for targets to be achieved is increasing then it could be decided to increase the time period between reviews.

Review meetings are likely to take a variety of formats. As discussed, in early years settings practitioners are likely to see family members on a regular basis, which will provide opportunities for informal discussion of progress. In addition though, it is good practice to hold review meetings where issues are discussed in a more systematic way. Review meetings may take place alongside other meetings, such as parent consultation evenings. This is completely acceptable, but it is important to ensure that there is ample time to discuss issues specifically related to IEP targets in enough depth. Consideration of when to hold a review meeting may also depend on availability of any external practitioners that are supporting the child or setting. To ensure that review meetings are effective it is useful to follow a set agenda. This will help to ensure that there is an opportunity for all parties to give their view, review the progress to date, discuss any changes that are needed and agree new targets.

To ensure that issues are followed up accurately and in a timely fashion it is important to think about how a record of the key points will be kept. Ideally this will be done during the meeting and relevant issues can be communicated to other practitioners who work with the child and necessary follow up action taken. Guidance from the DfES (2001d: 6) on what reviews should consider includes:

♦ the progress made by the child

♦ the parents' views (which includes all carers with parental responsibility)

♦ the child's view

♦ the effectiveness of the IEP

♦ any specific access issues that impact on a child's progress

♦ any updated information and advice

♦ further action, including changes to targets and strategies, addressing particular issues

♦ whether there is a need for more information or advice about the child, and how to access it.

Activity

Draft an agenda for a 30-minute review meeting. The agenda should aim to cover the range of areas suggested above and provide an opportunity for the child (either as part of the meeting or previous to the meeting), parents and practitioners to contribute to the meeting. An example of how this may look is included at the end of the chapter for you to compare with.

Who should write the IEP?

A final issue to consider with regards to IEPs is who writes them. It is neither realistic nor appropriate for a SENCO to have responsibility for writing all IEPs. As they should be seen as part of the ongoing planning process, the most appropriate person to write the IEP is the practitioner(s) who works directly with the child. In this way the IEP is more likely to be seen as a working document that practitioners can review and update on an ongoing basis. This does not mean that practitioners should be expected to write IEPs without support. The formal review of targets and setting of initial new targets will be informed by the review meeting process. If practitioners need further support, for example in devising different teaching strategies and approaches to differentiation it is important that you offer this as SENCO. Between formal reviews, external specialists may provide additional support and advice. For example, if a child has an autistic spectrum disorder, advice may come from a specialist advisory teacher and speech and language specialist. Again, part of the role of the SENCO is to ensure that practitioners have access to appropriate support and advice. This could be in the form of written communications and, where possible, face-to-face meetings. In this way, as SENCO, you will have an overview of what is occurring for all children who have a special educational need and will be able to provide support to colleagues to ensure that each child is able to make good progress. This will also help to ensure that your role as SENCO remains manageable but that you will continue to maintain an overview and coordinating role by supporting children, parents and colleagues.

An example of an agenda for a review meeting follows at the end of the chapter.

How does this agenda compare with yours? When constructing this agenda there were three central aims:

♦ to cover all of the issues that needed to be included in a review

♦ to ensure that decisions were made in the meeting based on feedback from all participants

♦ to keep the process efficient by allocating tasks during the meeting, ensuring that timescales were agreed and generating targets.

Based on their knowledge of what works for the child and the resources that are available, practitioners can add teaching approaches and strategies to the targets after the meeting.

Conclusion

This chapter has covered a range of issues related to the central role of IEPs in supporting children with SEN. The overall aim of this chapter was to show when it is necessary for a child to have an IEP, different approaches for providing IEPs for groups of children, how they can be devised and implemented, and strategies that can be applied to ensure that the child, family and all practitioners who support the child are involved in the process. This approach, as well as utilizing the skills of setting practitioners, will also ensure that effective communication is maintained with the family. The exemplar templates and activities within the chapter are intended to offer possible approaches to support SENCOs and early years settings in their roles, but need to be considered in the context of each setting.

Review Meeting Agenda

1. Introductions

   Distribute copies of previous IEP to guide discussion .... 1 minute

2. Feedback on agreed action points from last review meeting (if this has not been covered previously) ... 2 minutes

3. Comments from the child about whether they think they have achieved the targets (either direct or feedback from key worker) ... 4 minutes

4. Feedback from parents .... 5 minutes

5. Feedback from practitioners .... 5 minutes

6. Review of any information or advice received, and comments from external specialists if present.

   Are there any areas where additional advice is needed from other agencies? (This may be linked to a change in stage of SEN process.) ... 5 minutes

---

7. Drafting of next IEP targets based on feedback and discussion of the success of strategies and approaches used.

   Consideration of stage in SEN process – based on discussion and advice. Is a change needed?   5 minutes

8. Summary of agreed action points and timescales for completion   2 minutes

9. Agreement for date of next review based on rate of progress and discussion during meeting   1 minute

7

Devising Effective Administration Systems

It is possible to say with a degree of certainty that a SENCO will have to deal with a large amount of paperwork. In response to this it will be necessary to maintain a clear, accessible and informative record system to ensure that the setting offers effective support and provision for children with special needs. Recently there has been a push to reduce the amount of administration that SENCOs undertake and increase the time they spend on tasks that will benefit children (DfES 2004a). This is likely to lead to ongoing developments and the implementation of systems at local and national level, but it is still important to consider what developments you can make to systems within your setting. This chapter outlines some key considerations and approaches that can be used to support you in this aspect of your role.

Dealing with general administration

General administrative tasks include filing, letter writing, organizing meetings, reading about new developments and completing requests for documentation.

Devising Effective Administration Systems

A number of SENCOs feel challenged by the administrative demands of the post (Jones 2004). Perhaps the first important issue to agree within a setting is that it is not the role of the SENCO to deal with all aspects of administration. Firstly, it will be important to work with your colleagues and agree who will be responsible for different administrative tasks. Overall there will need to be clear systems in place for incoming information, dealing with information within the setting and outgoing information.

To manage, record and respond to each of these requests and ensure that effective systems are maintained it will be useful to consider the following points:

♦ Establish who will receive information initially and what will be done with it. To maintain an overview of incoming information and ensure that any follow up that is required is provided it may be better for the SENCO to see this before it is passed on to the relevant practitioners.

♦ Many requests that require a response may simply involve accessing information that is held centrally. For this to be effective it will be important to ensure there are consistent systems in place and that any administrative staff that assist the SENCO are aware of these systems.

♦ If information is required from practitioners, perhaps in response to an external request, it can be useful to provide a brief summary of what is required, when it is required by and who it should be returned to. This can be as simple as an attached memo that sets out the requirements and a summary of this can be noted on the SEN Overview Sheet (see Figure 7.1) to ensure that it is tracked and completed within the required timescale.

♦ It is likely that an individual file/record will be kept for each child with SEN or a disability. To ensure that this reflects past and current events a copy of all key documentation, information from other practitioners and correspondence should be kept. To assist with this it will be helpful to colleagues to have a central secure location where information can be stored.

Time allocation

In many early years settings and schools SENCOs do not have time allocated to the role. Quite simply, this is likely to impact on what can be achieved in the role. It would be inappropriate to suggest a recommended time allocation for the role but if *no* time is allocated this is an issue that should be raised with the management team. Time is important for carrying out the administrative aspects of the role, supporting colleagues and attending meetings. If time is allocated it is important to think carefully how it is used. It will need to be divided between each aspect of the role – if, for example, it is all allocated to attending meetings it will make the task of completing actions agreed in meetings difficult. As a SENCO it will be important to attend review meetings for children at Early Years Action and Early Years Action Plus stages of the SENCOP and this should be a priority in terms

Name	Area of SEN	Date SEN identified	Current stage	Date moved to stage	Previous stage	IEP review date	Notes

Figure 7.1 SEN Overview Sheet

of time management. It may not be necessary though to attend all meetings and such attendance should be agreed in discussion with the relevant practitioners. As mentioned earlier, other practitioners should be encouraged to see the contribution they can make as part of their role for children with SEN (e.g. writing IEPs and talking to other professionals who support the child). This sharing of responsibility will have four significant benefits. It will:

♦ ensure responsibilities are shared

♦ help with time demands

♦ give other practitioners opportunities to contribute to high-quality provision

♦ provide ongoing opportunities for continuing profes-sional development for all practitioners.

Communication

A key challenge in coordinating special needs processes is communication. To offer high-quality support for each child SENCOs need to communicate with a wide range of others, including colleagues, parents and other professionals. To manage this effectively and maintain good relationships it is important to consider what approaches will work in your setting. An important priority will be finding time to meet and discuss issues with each of these groups. Obviously, there will be times when plans will need to be altered to deal with issues quickly, but as far as possible it will help to set times aside for communication. To keep this aspect of the role manageable it will be helpful to think about:

♦ Implementing a system that allows you to offer support to colleagues at agreed times. For example, can meetings be arranged on a rota basis to coincide with any time allocation you have? In a school setting it may be possible to set aside regular time slots to communicate with colleagues during times when children are participating in group activities, such as assemblies.

♦ To communicate new developments or discuss procedures in your setting that involve all practitioners, try to communicate with all colleagues at the same time. This could be part of staff development and training sessions. It can also be useful to have SEN issues as a regular item on whole-staff meeting agendas to communicate necessary information.

♦ The majority of communication with parents is likely to take place with their child's key worker and other practitioners in their group or class. If there is a particular issue it is helpful to have a system where a parent(s) can book a time to meet with you.

♦ To maintain communication wherever possible, involve practitioners who work directly with the child in these meetings.

♦ To ensure that parents are aware of current plans it is helpful to send copies of IEPs or other relevant information. A covering letter (which can quickly be adapted from a standard template) to explain this is helpful to parents. This will take some time but this proactive approach will help to maintain a positive partnership and is likely to prevent problems occurring.

Tracking and monitoring systems

A key task for SENCOs is maintaining a clear overview for:

♦ drafting IEPs

♦ review meetings

♦ communicating with other people

♦ responding to requests for information

♦ attending necessary meetings

A tracking sheet (see Figure 7.1) is useful for this. This can hold details of each child who has an SEN and brief notes of current issues and actions to be completed. Using one overall sheet for this, will allow you to see at a glance upcoming issues and enable you to plan ahead accordingly. For this to be effective though it is important to update it on a regular basis. The time invested in this is likely to lead to better efficiency and less time needed in the future catching up with outstanding issues. For each child with SEN it is helpful to have an individual file. This should contain copies of IEPs, communication received and sent, and summary sheets from review meetings. An overview sheet, to record key events in date order, can also be useful to allow others to see at a glance past events, and can assist with completing requests that ask for an overview of what a setting has done to support a child.

Conclusion

If some of the approaches discussed are not in place it may appear that they would take a significant amount of time to devise, inform colleagues about and implement. However, this will be time well spent as the initial effort is likely to save time that is currently spent on dealing with administrative tasks. In addition, it will also be helpful to colleagues in establishing a consistent system, ensuring they are involved and providing them with relevant information to respond to any requests.

8

Multi-disciplinary Working and Supporting Transitions

Introduction

SENCOs work with colleagues from both within a setting and with other practitioners and agencies from outside the setting. These will include practitioners who regularly visit the setting to offer support to children, advice to practitioners and to meet with parents. Recently a number of children's centres have been established and these involve practitioners from a broad range of disciplines who will work in an interdisciplinary way. This chapter outlines how establishing effective joint working partnerships will support children during their transition into the setting, whilst at the setting and throughout their transition to the next phase of education.

Positive communication

A key aspect of creating an ethos of cooperation and responsiveness is to ensure there is clear communication. To achieve this requires opportunities for

---

Reflection

Think about a recent meeting or interaction with another person that was a positive experience. What made this a positive experience? If the scenario you have focused on included a commitment to carry out actions, were these completed?

---

all parties to express their view and be listened to. Of course, each interaction will vary but there are approaches that help to ensure effective communication. The following strategies, which you may have identified from the reflection activity, are helpful in achieving effective communication (Stuart 2003):

◆ Use positive nonverbal communication

◆ Avoid the use of technical jargon that other people may not understand

◆ Ask for clarification if there is something you do not understand

◆ Work with the person, not *on* the person

◆ Encourage each person to be frank and open

◆ Clarify any problems and take time to explore the whole range of possible solutions

◆ Be aware that people may come to issues with different value-bases. Try not to focus on this as it is usually not important

◆ Ensure that each person is clear about what they

have agreed to do and what the first steps are. It may help to record this in a written action plan.

Working with other services

Other professionals, such as health, portage and social services practitioners, can make a significant contribution to identifying and assessing SENs and providing support for children. This could include advice on physical, mental health, sensory impairments or communication difficulties. With the publication of the *National Service Framework for Children and Young People* there is a commitment to supporting children's mental well-being, and practitioners from Child and Adolescent Mental Health Services (CAMHS) will be able to provide advice on how to support children effectively (Department of Health 2004).

Young children may have had contact with practitioners from other services for a substantial time before entering an early years setting. To ensure a smooth transition into the setting it is important to work in partnership with these practitioners prior to a child starting and be guided by their advice. For a young child who is identified as having SEN during their time at a setting, it is worth considering whether informing the family's health visitor (after consultation with the family) could be helpful as multi-agency input in the early years is important. For children who have health problems they may have extended periods of time away from the setting. Effective partnership working and sharing of information with health practitioners will help to maintain an education input and a level of consistency for the child (DfES 2001f). For looked-after children it is vital to work with the child's social worker and ensure they are involved in all decisions (DfES 2001g).

When working with professionals who visit the setting, such as a speech and language therapist, it may be necessary to prioritize the children they work with. To respond to this it is helpful to consider, in discussion with the relevant professional, how different working patterns may be effective. For example, for children with less complex needs, the speech and language therapist could act in a consultancy role. This could involve them providing training for staff in the setting, advising on IEP targets and suggesting strategies that practitioners within the setting can implement when working with children. The multi-agency professional will then be able to work with children with more complex needs, whilst ensuring access to advice and support for all children. To achieve this flexible approach to working, time will need to be invested in developing positive relationships and all practitioners will need to be prepared to incorporate any newly agreed strategies into their working practice.

Transition planning

All children starting at a setting can find it a challenging time. If a child has SEN it can be particularly difficult. The transition will involve a whole range of issues that will have to be confronted, including:

♦ Getting to know a new set of practitioners and building trusting relationships with them

♦ Learning about the day-to-day working of the setting

♦ Responding to changes in the way learning is approached (particularly between the foundation stage and Key Stage 1)

♦ A change in (or possibly completely different) group of peers

♦ Learning about the way a setting provides for children with a SEN and the processes that occur with this.

Activity

Most settings will provide an information booklet for parents to tell them about many of these issues. Read through your booklet (or a booklet from a setting you are familiar with) and note what information it includes on supporting children with SEN. Does it address each of the points above? If not, spend some time amending it so that it provides the necessary information and is useful to all parents.

It is important to support children and families during the transition process. If a transition is taking place within the same setting (e.g. from nursery to a reception class or reception to Key Stage 1) parents may be more familiar with the overall ethos but will still need to know about differences in organization and approaches to practice. If a transition involves a child moving to a new setting, early planning and sharing of information will help to ensure this is a positive experience. To achieve this it is helpful to have a transition plan. This is something that is usually associated with the transition to secondary school, but elements of this can provide a good basis to ensure a smooth and successful transition for younger children too. To plan this will require cooperation between all practitioners who work with the child and parents (DfES 2001h). When constructing a transition plan it is useful to consider each of the following:

◆ How can the child be involved in the planning process and given an opportunity for their views to be heard?

◆ How can parents be fully involved in producing the plan?

◆ How can close working relationships with colleagues in other agencies be developed to ensure a successful transition?

◆ Do any new professionals need to be involved in the planning to support children in their new environment?

◆ Is there a clear procedure in place to transfer information to the new setting?

◆ Does the plan address the needs of the child in a holistic way?

Conclusion

This chapter has highlighted how effective working with multi-agency practitioners is vital to provide the best support for children. Multi-agency professionals will visit a number of settings and this emphasizes the need to take time to explain working practices from your setting so they feel welcome and a part of the team. To achieve this will require time and effort to be dedicated to forming relationships. The activities and suggestions in this chapter have set out approaches that can help to establish effective relationships and working practices between all practitioners.

Conclusion

It will be clear from reading this book that the role of the SENCO is complex but hopefully you will also feel that it offers significant opportunities for your own professional development, and in turn to ensure that children with SEN have a positive and stimulating early years experience. A significant amount of time will be spent supporting parents and working with multi-agency professionals. In reality, although these different aspects of the role are discussed in separate chapters of the book, they will often occur together. However, this should not be seen as problematic as the activities and discussions throughout the book will have assisted you in being reflective about these different parts of the role and will have suggested approaches to develop effective working practices. It will not be realistic to implement all of the suggested changes at once, but the book does provide a range of suggestions that you can draw on as needed to be able to respond competently and confidently to different situations.

The final activity in Chapter 1 asked you to review the different aspects of the SENCO role. After reading the book, it would be helpful to return to this activity and reflect on the action points you identified. The chapters in the second part of the book may well have provided some additional guidance that you can draw on to develop one or more parts of your action plan in more depth. You may feel that there is one particular area that you want to concentrate on developing as a priority, rather than focusing on all four. A key aim of the book is that it has been a useful tool in providing information and promoting reflection on your approach to special needs and the important contribution you can make to supporting children, parents and colleagues in the early years sector.

References

ACE bulletin (2003) *Avoiding Disability Discrimination*, 113. Advisory Centre for Education.

Adams, K.S. and Christenson, S.L. (2000) 'Trust and family–school relationship: examination of parent–teacher differences in elementary and secondary grades'. *Journal of School Psychology*, Vol. 38, No. 5, pp. 477–07.

Atkins, S. and Murphy, K. (1994) 'Reflective practice', *Nursing Standard*, Vol. 18, No. 39, pp. 49–54.

Baldock, P., Fitzgerald, D. and Kay, J. (2005) *Understanding Early Years Policy*. London: Paul Chapman.

Bruce, T. (1997) *Early Childhood Education (2nd edition)*. London: Hodder and Stoughton.

Bunt, G. (2001) 'The Special Educational Needs and Disability Act: the implications of PRS'. *PRS-LTSN Journal*, Vol. 1, No. 1, pp. 31–38.

Castle, A. (1996) 'Developing an ethos of reflective practice for continuing professional development'. *British Journal of Therapy and Rehabilitation*, Vol. 3, No. 7, pp. 358–59.

Chapoudy, R., Jameson, R. and Huber, P. (2001) 'Connecting families and schools through technology'. *Book Report*, Vol. 20, No. 2, pp. 52–57.

Children's Workforce Development Council (2006a) *CWDC – Developing the Early Years Workforce* [online]. Last accessed on 15 July 2006 at http://www.cwdcouncil.org.uk/projects/earlyyears.htm#Introduction

Children's Workforce Development Council (2006b) *Early Years Professional Prospectus*. Last accessed on 5 September 2006 at http://www.cwdcouncil.org.uk/pdf/Early%20Years/EYP_Prospectus_0806.pdf

Children's Workforce Development Council (2006c) *Draft Guidance to the Standards for the Award of Early Years Professional Status (Version 5)*. Last accessed on 5 September 2006 at http://www.cwdcouncil.org.uk/pdf/EYP%20Training%20Providers/Draft_Guidance_for_Phase_One_v5.pdf

Clark, A. (2004) 'The Mosaic Approach and Research with Young Children'. In Lewis, V., Kellett, M., Robinson, C., Fraser, S. and Ding, S. (eds) *The Reality of Research with Children and Young People*. London: Sage.

Cole, B.A. (2005) 'Mission impossible? Special educational needs, inclusion and the re-conceptualization of the role of the SENCO in England and Wales'. *European Journal of Special Needs Education*, Vol. 20, No. 3, pp. 287–307.

Cox, D.L. (2003) 'Wheelchair needs for children and young people: A review'. *British Journal of Occupational Therapy*, Vol. 66, No. 5, pp. 219–23.

Curtis, A. (1998) *A Curriculum for the Preschool Child (2nd edition)*. London: Routledge.

Department for Education (DfE) (1994) *Code of Practice for the Identification and Assessment of Special Educational Needs*. London: HMSO.

Department for Education and Skills (2001a) *Special*

Educational Needs Code of Practice. Nottingham: DfES.

Department for Education and Skills (2001b) *SEN Toolkit Section 1: Principles and Policies*. Nottingham: DfES.

Department for Education and Skills (2001c) *SEN Toolkit Section 4: Enabling Pupil Participation*. Nottingham: DfES.

Department for Education and Skills (2001d) *SEN Toolkit Section 5: Managing Individual Education Plans*. Nottingham: DfES.

Department for Education and Skills (2001e) *SEN Toolkit Section 4: Enabling Pupil Participation*. Nottingham: DfES.

Department for Education and Skills (2001f) *SEN Toolkit Section 12: The Role of Health Professionals*. Nottingham: DfES.

Department for Education and Skills (2001g) *SEN Toolkit Section 11: The Role of Social Services*. Nottingham: DfES.

Department for Education and Skills (2001h) *SEN Toolkit Section 10: Transition Planning*. Nottingham: DfES.

Department for Education and Skills (2004a) *Removing Barriers to Achievement: The Government's Strategy for SEN*. Nottingham: DfES.

Department for Education and Skills (2004b) *Every Child Matters: Next Steps* [online]. Last accessed on 30 June 2006 at http://www.everychildmatters.gov.uk_content/documents/EveryChildMattersNextSteps.pdf

Department for Education and Skills (2006) *Children's Workforce Strategy, Building a World-Class Workforce for Children, Young People and Families:*

The Government's Response to the Consultation [online]. Last accessed on 15 August 2006 at http://www.cwdcouncil.org.uk/resources/Every%20Child%20Matters%20-%20Change%20for%20Children.pdf

Department of Health (2004) *National Service Framework: Children, Young People and Maternity Services*. London: DoH.

Dewis, P. (2007) *Medical Conditions: A Guide for the Early Years*. London: Continuum.

Disability Rights Commission (2002) *Code of Practice for Schools (Disability Discrimination Act 1995, Part 4)*. London: HMSO.

Eldridge, D. (2001) 'Parental involvement: it's worth the effort'. *Young Children*, Vol. 56, No. 4, pp. 65–69.

Farrell, P. (2001) 'Special education in the last twenty years: have things really got better?' *British Journal of Special Education*, Vol. 28, No. 1, pp. 3–9.

Fazil, Q., Bywaters, P., Ali, Z., Wallace, L. and Singh, G. (2002) 'Disadvantage and discrimination compounded: the experience of Pakistani and Bangladeshi parents of disabled children in the UK'. *Disability and Society*, Vol. 17, No. 3, pp. 237–53.

Gerschel, L. (2005) 'The special educational needs coordinator's role in managing teaching assistants: the Greenwich perspective'. *Support for Learning*, Vol. 20, No. 2, pp. 69–76.

Greenman, J. (2001) 'Empowering parents'. *Childcare Information Exchange*, No. 138, pp. 56–59.

Hart, R. (1992) *Innocenti Essay (4): Children's Participation from Tokenism to Citizenship*. Florence: UNICEF.

Henshaw, L. (2003) 'Special educational needs and

the law: some practical implications'. *Education and the Law*, Vol. 15, No. 1, pp. 3–18.

Hilliard, D., Pelo, A. and Carter, M. (2001) 'Changing our attitude and actions in working with families'. *Childcare Information Exchange*, Vol. 138, pp. 48–51.

HM Treasury (2003) *Every Child Matters* (Cm. 5860) [online]. Last accessed on 15 June 2006 at http://everychildmatters.gov.uk/_content/documents/EveryChildMatters.pdf

HM Treasury/Department for Education and Skills/Department for Work and Pensions/Department of Trade and Industry (2004) *Choice for Parents, the Best Start for Children: A Ten-Year Strategy for Childcare*. London: HMSO.

Jones, C.A. (2004) *Supporting Inclusion in the Early Years*. Maidenhead: Open University Press.

Jordan, L., Reyes-Blanes, M.E., Peel, B.B., Peel, H.A. Lane, H.B. (1998) 'Developing teacher–parent partnerships across cultures: effective parent conferences'. *Intervention in School and Clinic*, Vol. 33, No. 3, pp. 141–42.

Kay, J. (2007) *Behavioural, Emotional and Social Difficulties: A Guide for the Early Years*. London: Continuum.

Kinrade, S. (2003) 'Working with patients: acting against discrimination'. *Professional Nurse*, Vol. 18, No. 2, pp. 714–15.

Kraft-Sayre, M.E. and Pianta, R.C. (2000) *Enhancing the Transition to Kindergarten*. Charlottesville: University of West Virginia, National Centre for Early Development and Learning.

Lawson, M.A. (2003) 'School–family relations in

context: parent and teacher perceptions of parental involvement'. *Urban Education*, Vol. 38, No. 1, pp. 77–133.

Layton, L. (2005) 'Special educational needs coordinators and leadership: a role too far?' *Support for Learning*, Vol. 20, No. 2, pp. 53–60.

Mackay, G. (2002) 'The disappearance of disability? Thoughts on a changing culture'. *British Journal of Special Education*, Vol. 29, No. 4, pp. 159–63.

Mackenzie, S. (2003) 'Parliamentary page'. *British Journal of Special Education*, Vol. 30, No. 3, pp. 164–66.

Miller, L., Cable, C. and Devereux, J. (2005) *Developing Early Years Practice*. London: David Fulton.

Northway, R. (2003) 'Valuing difference'. *Learning and Disability Practice*, Vol. 6, No. 9, p. 3.

Porter, L. (2002) *Educating Young Children with Special Needs*. London: Paul Chapman Publishing.

Riddell, S. (2003) 'Devolution and disability equality legislation: the implementation of Part 4 of the Disability Discrimination Act 1995 in England and Scotland'. *British Journal of Special Education*, Vol. 30, No. 2, pp. 63–69.

Rolfe, H., Metcalfe, H., Anderson, T. and Meadows, P. (2003) *Recruitment and Retention of Childcare, Early Years and Playworkers: Research Study*. National Institute of Economic and Social Research and Department for Education and Skills. London: HMSO.

Ofsted (Office for Standards in Education) (2001) *Full Day-Care: Guidance to the National Standards*. Nottingham: DfES.

O'Malley, K. (2004) *Children and Young People*

Participating in PRSP Processes: Lessons from Save the Children's experiences. London: Save the Children.

Qualifications and Curriculum Authority and Department for Education and Employment (2000) *Investing in Our Future: Curriculum Guidance for the Foundation Stage*. London: QCA: DfEE.

Schon, D. (1983) *The Reflective Practitioner: How Practitioners Think in Action*. New York: Basic Books.

Smith, F. and Barker, J. (2000) *Child Centred After School and Holiday Childcare: Final Report to the Economic and Social Research Council*. London: Brunnel University College.

Smith, F. and Barker, J. (2001) 'School's out? Out of school clubs at the boundary of home and school'. In Edwards, R. (ed) *Children, Home and School: Autonomy, Connection, or Regulation?* London: RoutledgeFalmer.

Smith, P.K., Cowie, H. and Blades, M. (2003) *Understanding Children's Development (4th edition)*. Oxford: Blackwell Publishing.

Special Educational Needs and Disability Tribunal (2003) Annual Report 2002–3. Last accessed on September 2006 at http://www.sendist.gov.uk/publications/documents/annual_report_2005.pdf

Special Educational Needs and Disability Tribunal (2005) Annual Report 2004–5. Last accessed on 18 April 2003 at http://www.sendist.gov.uk/uploads/AnnualReport2002-2003.pdf

Stewart, D., Law, M., Burke-Gaffney, J., Missiuna, C., Rosenbaum, P., King, G., Moning, T. and King, S. (2006) 'Keeping It Together: an information KIT for parents of children and youth with special needs'. *Child: Care, Health and Development*, Vol. 32, No. 4, pp. 493–500.

Stuart, C. (2003) *Assessment, Supervision and Support in Clinical Practice*. Edinburgh: Churchill Livingstone.

SureStart (2003) *Birth to Three Matters: A Framework to Support Children in their Earliest Years*. London: SureStart/DfES.

Sylva, K., Melhuish, E., Sammons, P., Siraj-Blatchford, I. and Taggart, B. (2004) *The Effective Provision of Pre-school Education (EPPE) Project: Findings from Pre-school to End of Key Stage One*. London: SureStart.

Teacher Development Agency for Schools (2006) *Draft Revised Standards for Teachers* [online]. Last accessed on 30 August 2006 at http://www.tda.gov.uk/upload/resources/pdf/d/draft_revised_standards_for_classroom_teachres_24_may_06.pdf

Teachernet (2006) *SEN Code of Practice from Teachernet* [online]. Last accessed on 31 August 2006 at http://www.teachernet.gov.uk/teachinginengland/detail.cfm?id=390

Thomas, N. (2001) 'Listening to Children'. In Foley, P., Roche, J. and Tucker, S. (eds) *Children in Society: Contemporary Theory, Policy and Practice*. Hampshire: Palgrave.

Treseder, P. (1997) *Empowering Children and Young People*. London: Save the Children.

UNICEF (1989) United Nations Convention for the Rights of the Child. Last accessed on 18 December 2006 at http://www.ohchr.org/english/law/pdf/crc.pdf

Unwin, K. (2005) 'Sharing support'. *Special Children*, January/February 2005, pp. 17–21.

Waterman, C. and Fowler, J. (2004) *Plain Guide to the Children Act 2004*. Berkshire: NFER.

Wenger, E. (1998) *Communities of Practice: Learning, Meaning and Identity*. Cambridge: Cambridge University Press.

Whalley, M. (2001) *Involving Parents in their Children's Learning*. London: Paul Chapman.

Wyse, D. (2004) 'Research with children'. In Wyse, D. (ed) *Childhood Studies: An Introduction*. Oxford: Blackwell Publishing.